CONTEMPORARY
AMERICAN
POETRY

LITERARY HERITAGE

A Macmillan Paperback Series

Advisory Editorial Board

Dora V. Smith
Joseph Mersand
James Squire

GENERAL EDITOR
Marjorie Wescott Barrows

CONTEMPORARY
AMERICAN
POETRY

H. Lincoln Foster
Housatonic Valley Regional High School
Falls Village, Connecticut

The Macmillan Company, New York

ACKNOWLEDGMENTS

For permission to use the poems in this book grateful acknowledgment is made to the following:

Curtis Brown, Ltd.: For "A Caution to Everybody," from *Private Dining Room and Other Verses*, by Ogden Nash. Reprinted by permission of the author. Copyright © 1950 by Ogden Nash.

Norma Millay Ellis: For "Northern April," "Pity Me Not Because the Light of Day," "I Shall Go Back Again," "Love, Though for This You Riddle Me with Darts," "Song of a Second April," "God's World," "Renascence," "The Unexplorer," and "Elegy," by Edna St. Vincent Millay, from *Collected Poems*, Harper & Brothers, copyright 1912-1913-1920-1921-1922-1923-1928-1940-1947-1948-1950-1951-1955 by Edna St. Vincent Millay and Norma Millay Ellis.

Grove Press, Inc.: For "Oread," "Orchard," and "Heat" (Part Two of "The Garden") by H.D., from *H.D. Selected Poems*, published by Grove Press, Inc.; copyright © 1957 by Norman Holmes Pearson.

Harcourt, Brace & World, Inc.: For "Still, Citizen Sparrow" and "Museum Piece," by Richard Wilbur, from *Ceremony and Other Poems*; copyright, 1948, 1949, 1950, by Richard Wilbur. For "Year's-End" and "Juggler," by Richard Wilbur, from *Ceremony and Other Poems*; copyright, 1949, by Richard Wilbur. For "The Beautiful Changes," by Richard Wilbur, from *The Beautiful Changes*; copyright, 1947, by Richard Wilbur. For "Threes," from *Smoke and Steel*, by Carl Sandburg; copyright, 1920, by Harcourt, Brace & World, Inc., renewed, 1948, by Carl Sandburg. For "The People Will Live On," from *The People, Yes*, by Carl Sandburg; copyright, 1936, by Harcourt, Brace & World, Inc. For "Spring is like a perhaps hand," by E. E. Cummings, copyright 1925 by E. E. Cummings; "Buffalo Bill's," by E. E. Cummings, copyright 1923, 1951 by E. E. Cummings; "what if a much of a which of a wind" and "pity this busy monster, manunkind," by E. E. Cummings, copyright 1944 by E. E. Cummings; all from *Poems 1923-1954*, by E. E. Cummings. All reprinted by permission of Harcourt, Brace & World, Inc.

Holt, Rinehart and Winston, Inc.: For "Speech to Those Who Say Comrade," from *Public Speech*, by Archibald MacLeish. Copyright 1936 by Archibald MacLeish. For "Chicago" and "Happiness," from *Chicago Poems*, by Carl Sandburg; copyright 1916 by Holt, Rinehart and Winston, Inc., copyright renewed 1944 by Carl Sandburg. For "Psalm of Those Who Go Forth Before Daylight" and "Cool Tombs," from *Cornhuskers*, by Carl Sandburg; copyright 1918 by Holt, Rinehart and Winston, Inc., copyright renewed 1946 by Carl Sandburg. For "Into My Own," "A Prayer in Spring," "The Tuft of Flowers," "In Hardwood Groves," "Reluctance," "Mending Wall," "Home Burial," "After Apple-Picking," "The Exposed Nest," "Dust of Snow," "Sand Dunes," "On Looking Up by Chance at the Constellations," "Two Tramps in Mud Time," "The White-Tailed Hornet," "At Woodward's Gardens," "A Record Stride," "The Gift Outright," and "Triple Bronze," from *Complete Poems of Robert Frost*; copyright 1916, 1921, 1923, 1928, 1930, 1939, 1944 by Holt, Rine-

CONTENTS

Foreword

During the first half of the twentieth century there were more American writers seriously devoting themselves to poetry than at any previous time in the country's literary history. The general quality of this poetry was good, and it represented a wide diversity of styles. This very quality and diversity have made it difficult, even for critics and scholars, to trace the development of modern poetry in America. Certain stages and directions, however, can be suggested.

During the nineteenth century the poets of the New England tradition did much to give American literature a reputation in the English-speaking world. Longfellow, Whittier, Bryant, Holmes, Emerson, and others presented American subject matter in a style modeled on traditional English poetry. About the same time, four poets who did not belong to this New England tradition were experimenting with new subject matter and techniques; namely, Whitman, Poe, Lanier, and Emily Dickinson. All wrote in styles so different from the then-popular style that they had little influence on American poetry until they were rediscovered by the poets of the twentieth century.

During the final decades of the nineteenth century and the first decade of the twentieth century, America could boast of no new major poets. The literary scene was dominated by prose writers concerned with man's struggle against the indifferent forces of nature and of society.

To some extent, the young poets of this period were influenced by the prose literature of realism and social protest, but until the founding, in 1912, of *Poetry: A Magazine of Verse*, there was little opportunity for these poets to publish their works. The originator of this magazine was Miss Harriet Monroe, also a poet, and from the beginning *Poetry* was an extraordinary success. It attracted as contributors the young poets who were experimenting in many different ways with the form and content of poetry. Their experiments provoked much controversy, and the magazine soon became the battleground for arguments about the nature and craft of poetry. The so-called "New Poetry" became such a popular subject of debate that it was discussed even in the columns of daily newspapers. What mattered most was that poetry was being read by an ever-increasing audience. The result was a reawakening of creative expression and the encouragement of experimentation.

CONTEMPORARY
AMERICAN
POETRY

THE TRADITIONALISTS

THE traditionalists among the major contemporary poets of America are traditional only in form and technique. Their stanzas and meters and rhymes have a familiar look, for, like the nineteenth-century New England poets, the traditionalists have made use of such long-established verse forms as blank verse, rhymed couplet, quatrain, and sonnet. What marks them as modern poets is what they have written about, their attitude toward it, and the language they have employed.

To be sure, the traditionalists have written many poems about such familiar subjects as death, love, and nature, but the way in which they have presented these subjects is new and different. Instead of expressing general and romantic sentiments about life and nature, these poets have revealed their thoughts, feelings, and impressions in highly personalized experiences. When E. A. Robinson wrote about death, it was about the death of a particular person, a Richard Cory or a Lorraine. When Edna St. Vincent Millay wrote of love, it was about a particular moment of joy, grief, or despair. When Robert Frost wrote of nature, it was of a specific time and place: a particular hardwood grove, a personal experience in a flowery meadow. In the works of all these poets the stuff of everyday experience is made as personal and immediate for the reader as first-hand experience itself. Instead of writing *about* a deeply felt emotion, they have evoked it *through* impressions and images that capture the reader's imagination.

Furthermore, these modern traditionalists frequently explored aspects of life that one rarely finds mentioned in the romantic poetry of the early New England poets. Even the uglier features of rural and urban life are pictured realistically, though not to the extent that they are pictured by the poets who later experimented with the *forms* of American poetry. What distinguishes the traditionalists is the language they used in their poems. It is much closer to the language of prose and of everyday speech than to the special language of poetry so popular in the nineteenth century. Rarely will you find such "poetic" expressions as "Thou layest thy finger on the lips of Care." Nor will you find as many inversions of word order such as "Thou, in sunny solitudes, the green silence dost displace." In elements of form, regular meter, rhyme, and stanza patterns, these poets of the early twentieth century are essentially traditional. In subject matter, in tone, and especially in language, they are essentially modern.

Edwin Arlington Robinson

The poetry of Edwin Arlington Robinson reflects a sensitive, inquiring mind probing beneath the surface of human action and human motives. Though a tone of pessimism runs through much of Robinson's poetry, he does reveal a deep love of human beings and an admiration for the human spirit which battles against the horrors and contradictions of life.

Robinson wrote many long narrative poems rich in insight into the workings of the human mind and heart. Whether he based his narrative on the events and characters of the Arthurian legends or on a contemporary story full of moral conflict, he developed the full drama of events and interplay of character. Even in his sonnets and shorter traditional verses, emotional tension arises from his exploration of the human heart. The language and imagery of his poetry are always secondary to the ideas he wanted to express; they are precise tools, never strange and flashy for their own sake.

Richard Cory

Whenever Richard Cory went down town,
We people on the pavement looked at him:
He was a gentleman from sole to crown,
Clean favored, and imperially slim.

And he was always quietly arrayed, 5
And he was always human when he talked;
But still he fluttered pulses when he said,
"Good-morning," and he glittered when he walked.

And he was rich—yes, richer than a king—
And admirably schooled in every grace: 10
In fine, we thought that he was everything
To make us wish that we were in his place.

So on we worked, and waited for the light,
And went without the meat, and cursed the bread;
And Richard Cory, one calm summer night,   15
Went home and put a bullet through his head.

1. What qualities of character are emphasized in stanzas 1-3? Through
    whose eyes are these seen? Note the words and phrases used. Tell
    why you think they do, or do not, suggest an aloof and haughty person.
2. How is the language in lines 15 and 16 different from that in the rest
    of the poem? What effect does this have on the meaning? If you had
    been told why Richard Cory committed suicide, would the total effect
    of the poem have been different? Explain.

The Growth of "Lorraine"

I

While I stood listening, discreetly dumb,
Lorraine was having the last word with me:
"I know," she said, "I know it, but you see
Some creatures are born fortunate, and some
Are born to be found out and overcome,—   5
Born to be slaves, to let the rest go free;
And if I'm one of them (and I must be)
You may as well forget me and go home.

"You tell me not to say these things, I know,
But I should never try to be content: 10
I've gone too far; the life would be too slow.
Some could have done it—some girls have the stuff;
But I can't do it: I don't know enough.
I'm going to the devil."—And she went.

II

I did not half believe her when she said   15
That I should never hear from her again;
Nor when I found a letter from Lorraine,
Was I surprised or grieved at what I read:
"Dear friend, when you find this, I shall be dead.
You are too far away to make me stop.   20
They say that one drop—think of it, one drop!—
Will be enough,—but I'll take five instead.

"You do not frown because I call you friend,
For I would have you glad that I still keep
Your memory, and even at the end—   25
Impenitent, sick, shattered—cannot curse
The love that flings, for better or for worse,
This worn-out, cast-out flesh of mine to sleep."

1. What meaning do you think the poet intended to convey by the word
   growth in the title? What was Lorraine's opinion of herself? How do
   you interpret lines 13-14?
2. In Part I, what clues suggest the relationship between the speaker
   and Lorraine? What do you learn about her behavior that would lead
   the young man to say that he was not surprised at her letter?
3. Lorraine's "suicide note" would suggest that this was a poem of
   tragedy. What evidence in the poem suggests that it was or was not?
   Are Lorraine's remarks at the end of the poem consistent with her
   remarks in Part I? Explain.
4. Plot the rhyme scheme and the meter of the two sections. In what
   ways are the two parts alike and in what ways different? Into what
   kind of traditional poetic form does each part fall? In Part I which
   phrases, by their double meaning, give humor to the poem?

Cassandra[1]

I heard one who said: "Verily,
    What word have I for children here?
Your Dollar is your only Word,
    The wrath of it your only fear.

"You build it altars tall enough   5
    To make you see, but you are blind;
You cannot leave it long enough
    To look before you or behind.

"When Reason beckons you to pause,
    You laugh and say that you know best;   10
But what it is you know, you keep
    As dark as ingots in a chest.

"You laugh and answer, 'We are young;
    O leave us now, and let us grow.'—
Not asking how much more of this   15
    Will Time endure or Fate bestow.

"Because a few complacent years
    Have made your peril of your pride,
Think you that you are to go on
    Forever pampered and untried?   20

"What lost eclipse of history,
    What bivouac° of the marching stars,   stopping
Has given the sign for you to see
    Millenniums[2] and last great wars?

---

[1] *Cassandra*, a prophetess who was never believed

[2] *Millenniums. Revelations* refers to the millennium—a thousand years when holiness will prevail in the world.

"What unrecorded overthrow   25
    Of all the world has ever known,
Or ever been, has made itself
    So plain to you, and you alone?

"Your Dollar, Dove and Eagle make
    A Trinity that even you   30
Rate higher than you rate yourselves;
    It pays, it flatters, and it's new.

"And though your very flesh and blood
    Be what your Eagle eats and drinks,
You'll praise him for the best of birds,   35
    Not knowing what the Eagle thinks.

"The power is yours, but not the sight;
    You see not upon what you tread;
You have the ages for your guide,
    But not the wisdom to be led.   40

"Think you to tread forever down
    The merciless old verities?°   truths
And are you never to have eyes
    To see the world for what it is?

"Are you to pay for what you have   45
    With all you are?"—No other word
We caught, but with a laughing crowd
    Moved on. None heeded, and few heard.

1. Who spoke the words which the poet heard (note line 1)? What is
   implied in line 2 by the word *children?* Why is *Word* capitalized in
   line 3? To what does *it* refer in stanza 2?
2. What reason do the people give for ignoring Reason? With what
   doom are they threatened? (See stanza 4.) Where else in the poem
   is this doom foretold? What is the meaning of stanzas 6 and 7? What
   is the poet's attitude—tone of voice—in these two stanzas?
3. The Dollar, Dove, and Eagle are referred to as a Trinity. Why? What
   does each of the three symbolize? What specific stanzas refer to each?

In lines 45 and 46, what error in values is suggested? What specific illustrations of the error can you find in the poem? What evidence can you find that "none heeded and few heard" Cassandra's warnings?

Credo

I cannot find my way: there is no star
In all the shrouded heavens anywhere;
And there is not a whisper in the air
Of any living voice but one so far
That I can hear it only as a bar   5
Of lost, imperial music, played when fair
And angel fingers wove, and unaware,
Dead leaves to garlands where no roses are.

No, there is not a glimmer, nor a call,
For one that welcomes, welcomes when he fears,   10
The black and awful chaos of the night;
For through it all—above, beyond it all—
I know the far-sent message of the years,
I feel the coming glory of the Light.

1. Why was the speaker in the poem unable to find his way? What does "the way" represent? What do the images suggested by star (line 1) and whisper (line 3) represent? In what lines are these images used again? What is the "lost, imperial music"? How do you interpret line 8?
2. Why does the speaker welcome, "when he fears, the black and awful chaos of the night"? What faith supports him?

The Children of the Night

For those that never know the light,
  The darkness is a sullen thing;
And they, the Children of the Night,
  Seem lost in Fortune's winnowing.°   sifting good from bad

But some are strong and some are weak,—   5
  And there's the story. House and home
Are shut from countless hearts that seek
  World-refuge that will never come.

And if there be no other life,
  And if there be no other chance   10
To weigh their sorrow and their strife
  Than in the scales of circumstance,

'Twere better, ere the sun go down
  Upon the first day we embark,
In life's imbittered sea to drown,   15
  Than sail forever in the dark.

But if there be a soul on earth
  So blinded with its own misuse
Of man's revealed, incessant worth,
  Or worn with anguish, that it views   20

No light but for a mortal eye,
  No rest but of a mortal sleep,
No God but in a prophet's lie,
  No faith for "honest doubt" to keep;

If there be nothing, good or bad,   25
  But chaos for a soul to trust,—

God counts it for a soul gone mad,
   And if God be God, He is just.

And if God be God, He is Love;
   And though the Dawn be still so dim,   30
It shows us we have played enough
   With creeds that make a friend of Him.

There is one creed, and only one,
   That glorifies God's excellence;
So cherish, that His will be done,   35
   The common creed of common sense.

It is the crimson, not the gray,
   That charms the twilight of all time;
It is the promise of the day
   That makes the starry sky sublime;   40

It is the faith within the fear
   That holds us to the life we curse;—
So let us in ourselves revere
   The Self which is the Universe!

Let us, the Children of the Night,   45
   Put off the cloak that hides the scar!
Let us be Children of the Light,
   And tell the ages what we are!

1. Who are "the Children of the Night"? What do you learn about them in stanzas 1 and 2? Do you think they were victims of chance? If so, what did the speaker in the poem suggest was the only solution to their plight?
2. What kind of person is characterized in stanzas 5, 6, and 7? How do you interpret stanza 8?
3. What is the "one creed" that "glorifies God's excellence"? How is it related to the ideas presented in stanzas 10 and 11, and particularly to lines 43 and 44?
4. In the last stanza, what message did the author have for us, "the Children of the Night"? What do the cloak and the scar symbolize? How do you interpret the last line of the poem?

5. Point out the images in stanza 10 that are used with variations throughout the poem. Also point out the phrases which provide clues to the
   meaning of these images.

Ben Jonson Entertains a Man from Stratford

You are a friend then, as I make it out,
Of our man Shakespeare, who alone of us
Will put an ass's head in Fairyland
As he would add a shilling to more shillings,
All most harmonious,—and out of his   5
Miraculous inviolable increase°   unending supply
Fills Ilion, Rome, or any town you like
Of olden time with timeless Englishmen;
And I must wonder what you think of him—
All you down there where your small Avon flows   10
By Stratford, and where you're an Alderman.
Some, for a guess, would have him riding back
To be a farrier° there, or say a dyer;   horseshoer
Or maybe one of your adept surveyors;
Or like enough the wizard of all tanners.   15
Not you—no fear of that; for I discern
In you a kindling of the flame that saves—
The nimble element, the true caloric;°   warmth
I see it, and was told of it, moreover,
By our discriminate friend himself, no other.   20
Had you been one of the sad average,
As he would have it,—meaning, as I take it,
The sinew and the solvent° of our Island,   life-blood
You'd not be buying beer for this Terpander's[1]
Approved and estimated friend Ben Jonson;   25
He'd never foist° it as a part of his   impose
Contingent entertainment of a townsman
While he goes off rehearsing, as he must,
If he shall ever be the Duke of Stratford.

---

[1] *Terpander*, regarded as the founder of Greek lyric poetry

And my words are no shadow on your town—   30
Far from it; for one town's as like another
As all are unlike London. Oh, he knows it,—
And there's the Stratford in him; he denies it,
And there's the Shakespeare in him. So, God help him!
I tell him he needs Greek; but neither God   35
Nor Greek will help him. Nothing will help that man.
You see the fates have given him so much,
He must have all or perish,—or look out
Of London, where he sees too many lords.
They're part of half what ails him: I suppose   40
There's nothing fouler down among the demons
Than what it is he feels when he remembers
The dust and sweat and ointment of his calling
With his lords looking on and laughing at him.
King as he is, he can't be king *de facto*,[2]   45
And that's as well, because he wouldn't like it;
He'd frame a lower rating of men then
Than he has now; and after that would come
An abdication or an apoplexy.
He can't be king, not even king of Stratford,—   50
Though half the world, if not the whole of it,
May crown him with a crown that fits no king
Save Lord Apollo's[3] homesick emissary:°   agent
Not there on Avon, or on any stream
Where Naiads[4] and their white arms are no more,   55
Shall he find home again. It's all too bad.
But there's a comfort, for he'll have that House—
The best you ever saw; and he'll be there
Anon, as you're an Alderman. Good God!
He makes me lie awake o'nights and laugh.   60

And you have known him from his origin,
You tell me; and a most uncommon urchin
He must have been to the few seeing ones—

---
[2] *de facto*, in reality
[3] *Apollo*, god of song and poetry
[4] *Naiads*, water nymphs

A trifle terrifying, I dare say,
Discovering a world with his man's eyes,   65
Quite as another lad might see some finches,
If he looked hard and had an eye for nature.
But this one had his eyes and their foretelling.
And he had you to fare with, and what else!
He must have had a father and a mother—   70
In fact I've heard him say so—and a dog,
As a boy should, I venture; and the dog,
Most likely, was the only man who knew him.
A dog, for all I know, is what he needs
As much as anything right here to-day,   75
To counsel him about his disillusions,
Old aches, and parturitions° of what's coming,—   pangs
A dog of orders,° an emeritus,°   honors; a retired dignitary
To wag his tail at him when he comes home,
And then to put his paws up on his knees   80
And say, "For God's sake, what's it all about?"

I don't know whether he needs a dog or not—
Or what he needs. I tell him he needs Greek;
I'll talk of rules and Aristotle[5] with him,
And if his tongue's at home he'll say to that,   85
"I have your word that Aristotle knows,
And you mine that I don't know Aristotle."
He's all at odds with all the unities,[6]
And what's yet worse, it doesn't seem to matter;
He treads along through Time's old wilderness   90
As if the tramp of all the centuries
Had left no roads—and there are none, for him;
He doesn't see them, even with those eyes,—
And that's a pity, or I say it is.
Accordingly we have him as we have him—   95
Going his way, the way that he goes best,
A pleasant animal with no great noise
Or nonsense anywhere to set him off—

---

[5] *Aristotle*, author of the *Poetics*, a book of rules for Greek poetic drama
[6] *unities*. Aristotle urged dramatists to observe unity of time, place, and action.

Save only divers° and inclement° devils   varied; rough
Have made of late his heart their dwelling place.   100
A flame half ready to fly out sometimes
At some annoyance may be fanned up in him,
But soon it falls, and when it falls goes out;
He knows how little room there is in there
For crude and futile animosities,   105
And how much for the joy of being whole,
And how much for long sorrow and old pain.
On our side there are some who may be given°   disposed
To grow old wondering what he thinks of us
And some above us, who are, in his eyes,   110
Above himself,—and that's quite right and English.
Yet here we smile, or disappoint the gods
Who made it so: the gods have always eyes
To see men scratch; and they see one down here
Who itches, manor-bitten° to the bone,   house-hungry 115
Albeit° he knows himself—yes, yes, he knows—   although
The lord of more than England and of more
Than all the seas of England in all time
Shall ever wash. D'ye wonder that I laugh?
He sees me, and he doesn't seem to care;   120
And why the devil should he? I can't tell you.

I'll meet him out alone of a bright Sunday,
Trim, rather spruce, and quite the gentleman.
"What ho, my lord!" say I. He doesn't hear me;
Wherefore I have to pause and look at him.   125
He's not enormous, but one looks at him.
A little on the round if you insist,
For now, God save the mark, he's growing old;
He's five and forty, and to hear him talk
These days you'd call him eighty; then you'd add   130
More years to that. He's old enough to be
The father of a world, and so he is.
"Ben, you're a scholar, what's the time of day?"
Says he; and there shines out of him again
An aged light that has no age or station—   135

The mystery that's his—a mischievous
Half-mad serenity that laughs at fame
For being won so easy, and at friends
Who laugh at him for what he wants the most,
And for his dukedom down in Warwickshire;—   140
By which you see we're all a little jealous. . . .
Poor Greene![7] I fear the color of his name
Was even as that of his ascending soul;
And he was one where there are many others,—
Some scrivening° to the end against their fate,   writing 145
Their puppets all in ink and all to die there;
And some with hands that once would shade an eye
That scanned Euripides and Æschylus[8]
Will reach by this time for a pot-house° mop   tavern
To slush their first and last of royalties.°   payments for plays 150
Poor devils! and they all play to his hand;
For so it was in Athens and old Rome.
But that's not here or there; I've wandered off.
Greene does it, or I'm careful. Where's that boy?

Yes, he'll go back to Stratford. And we'll miss him?   155
Dear sir, there'll be no London here without him.
We'll all be riding, one of these fine days,
Down there to see him—and his wife won't like us;
And then we'll think of what he never said
Of women—which, if taken all in all   160
With what he did say, would buy many horses.
Though nowadays he's not so much for women:
"So few of them," he says, "are worth the guessing."
But there's a worm at work when he says that,
And while he says it one feels in the air   165
A deal of circumambient° hocus-pocus.   roundabout
They've had him dancing till his toes were tender,
And he can feel 'em now, come chilly rains.
There's no long cry for going into it,
However, and we don't know much about it.   170

---

[7] Greene, Elizabethan dramatist, killed in a tavern brawl
[8] Euripides and Æschylus, Greek dramatists

But you in Stratford, like most here in London,
Have more now in the *Sonnets*[9] than you paid for;
He's put one there with all her poison on,
To make a singing fiction of a shadow
That's in his life a fact, and always will be.   175
But she's no care of ours, though Time, I fear,
Will have a more reverberant ado
About her than about another one
Who seems to have decoyed him, married him,
And sent him scuttling on his way to London,—   180
With much already learned, and more to learn,
And more to follow. Lord! how I see him now,
Pretending, maybe trying, to be like us.
Whatever he may have meant, we never had him;
He failed us, or escaped, or what you will,—   185
And there was that about him (God knows what,—
We'd flayed° another had he tried it on us)   criticized
That made as many of us as had wits
More fond of all his easy distances
Than one another's noise and clap-your-shoulder.   190
But think you not, my friend, he'd never talk!
Talk? He was eldritch° at it; and we listened—   uncanny
Thereby acquiring much we knew before
About ourselves, and hitherto had held
Irrelevant, or not prime to the purpose.   195
And there were some, of course, and there be now,
Disordered and reduced amazedly
To resignation by the mystic seal
Of young finality the gods had laid
On everything that made him a young demon;   200
And one or two shot looks at him already
As he had been their executioner;
And once or twice he was, not knowing it,—
Or knowing, being sorry for poor clay
And saying nothing. . . . Yet, for all his engines,°   rare abilities 205
You'll meet a thousand of an afternoon
Who strut and sun themselves and see around 'em
A world made out of more that has a reason

---

[9] *Sonnets*, a reference to the "dark lady" whose identity is uncertain

Than his, I swear, that he sees here to-day;
Though he may scarcely give a Fool° an exit   *jester* 210
But we mark° how he sees in everything   *notice*
A law that, given we flout° it once too often,   *sneer at*
Brings fire and iron down on our naked heads.
To me it looks as if the power that made him,
For fear of giving all things to one creature,   215
Left out the first,—faith, innocence, illusion,
Whatever 'tis that keeps us out o' Bedlam,¹⁰—
And thereby, for his too consuming vision,
Empowered him out of nature; though to see him,
You'd never guess what's going on inside him.   220
He'll break out some day like a keg of ale
With too much independent frenzy in it;
And all for cellaring what he knows won't keep,
And what he'd best forget—but that he can't.
You'll have it, and have more than I'm foretelling;   225
And there'll be such a roaring at the Globe
As never stunned the bleeding gladiators.
He'll have to change the color of its hair
A bit, for now he calls it Cleopatra.
Black hair would never do for Cleopatra.   230
But you and I are not yet two old women,
And you're a man of office. What he does
Is more to you than how it is he does it,—
And that's what the Lord God has never told him.
They work together, and the Devil helps 'em;   235
They do it of a morning, or if not,
They do it of a night; in which event
He's peevish of a morning. He seems old;
He's not the proper stomach or the sleep—
And they're two sovran° agents to conserve him   *excellent* 240
Against the fiery art that has no mercy
But what's in that prodigious grand new House.
I gather something happening in his boyhood
·Fulfilled him with a boy's determination
To make all Stratford 'ware of him. Well, well,   245
I hope at last he'll have his joy of it,

---

¹⁰ *Bedlam*, London insane asylum

And all his pigs and sheep and bellowing beeves,
And frogs and owls and unicorns, moreover,
Be less than hell to his attendant ears.
Oh, past a doubt we'll all go down to see him.   250

He may be wise. With London two days off,
Down there some wind of heaven may yet revive him;
But there's no quickening breath from anywhere
Shall make of him again the poised young faun
From Warwickshire, who'd made, it seems, already   255
A legend of himself before I came
To blink before the last of his first lightning.
Whatever there be, there'll be no more of that;
The coming on of his old monster Time
Has made him a still man; and he has dreams   260
Were fair to think on once, and all found hollow.
He knows how much of what men paint themselves
Would blister in the light of what they are;
He sees how much of what was great now shares
An eminence° transformed and ordinary;   greatness 265
He knows too much of what the world has hushed
In others, to be loud now for himself;
He knows now at what height low enemies
May reach his heart, and high friends let him fall;
But what not even such as he may know   270
Bedevils him the worst: his lark may sing
At heaven's gate how he will, and for as long
As joy may listen, but *he* sees no gate,
Save one whereat the spent clay waits a little
Before the churchyard has it, and the worm.   275
Not long ago, late in an afternoon,
I came on him unseen down Lambeth way,
And on my life I was afear'd of him:
He gloomed and mumbled like a soul from Tophet,°   hell
His hands behind him and his head bent solemn.   280
"What is it now," said I,—"another woman?"
That made him sorry for me, and he smiled.
"No, Ben," he mused; "it's Nothing. It's all Nothing.
We come, we go; and when we're done, we're done.
Spiders and flies—we're mostly one or t'other—   285

We come, we go; and when we're done, we're done."
"By God, you sing that song as if you knew it!"
Said I, by way of cheering him; "what ails ye?"
"I think I must have come down here to think,"
Says he to that, and pulls his little beard;   290
"Your fly will serve as well as anybody,
And what's his hour? He flies, and flies, and flies,
And in his fly's mind has a brave appearance;
And then your spider gets him in her net,
And eats him out, and hangs him up to dry.   295
That's Nature, the kind mother of us all.
And then your slattern housemaid swings her broom,
And where's your spider? And that's Nature, also.
It's Nature, and it's Nothing. It's all Nothing.
It's all a world where bugs and emperors   300
Go singularly° back to the same dust,   strangely
Each in his time; and the old, ordered stars
That sang together, Ben, will sing the same
Old stave° to-morrow."   set of verses

         When he talks like that,   305
There's nothing for a human man to do
But lead him to some grateful° nook like this   welcome
Where we be now, and there to make him drink.
He'll drink, for love of me, and then be sick;
A sad sign always in a man of parts,°   abilities 310
And always very ominous. The great
Should be as large in liquor as in love,—
And our great friend is not so large in either:
One disaffects° him, and the other fails him;   upsets
Whatso he drinks that has an antic° in it,   mocking spirit 315
He's wondering what's to pay in his insides;
And while his eyes are on the Cyprian[11]
He's fribbling° all the time with that damned House.   toying
We laugh here at his thrift, but after all
It may be thrift that saves him from the devil;   320
God gave it, anyhow,—and we'll suppose
He knew the compound of his handiwork.
To-day the clouds are with him, but anon

---

[11] Cyprian, a reference to Aphrodite, goddess of love

He'll out of 'em enough to shake the tree
Of life itself and bring down fruit unheard-of,—   325
And, throwing in the bruised and whole together,
Prepare a wine to make us drunk with wonder;
And if he live, there'll be a sunset spell
Thrown over him as over a glassed lake
That yesterday was all a black wild water.   330

God send he live to give us, if no more,
What now's a-rampage° in him, and exhibit,   raging
With a decent half-allegiance to the ages
An earnest° of at least a casual eye   token
Turned once on what he owes to Gutenberg,[12]   335
And to the fealty° of more centuries   steadfast devotion
Than are as yet a picture in our vision.
"There's time enough,—I'll do it when I'm old,
And we're immortal men," he says to that;
And then he says to me, "Ben, what's 'immortal'?   340
Think you by any force of ordination°   God's will
It may be nothing of a sort more noisy
Than a small oblivion of component ashes
That of a dream-addicted world was once
A moving atomy° much like your friend here?"   skeleton   345
Nothing will help that man. To make him laugh,
I said then he was a mad mountebank,°—   fake
And by the Lord I nearer made him cry.
I could have eat an eft° then, on my knees,   small salamander
Tail, claws, and all of him; for I had stung   350
The king of men, who had no sting for me,
And I had hurt him in his memories;
And I say now, as I shall say again,
I love the man this side idolatry.

He'll do it when he's old, he says. I wonder.   355
He may not be so ancient as all that.
For such as he, the thing that is to do
Will do itself,—but there's a reckoning;
The sessions that are now too much his own,

[12] Gutenberg, inventor of the printing press

The roiling° inward of a stilled outside,   turbulence 360
The churning out of all those blood-fed lines,
The nights of many schemes and little sleep,
The full brain hammered hot with too much thinking,
The vexed heart over-worn with too much aching,—
This weary jangling of conjoined affairs   365
Made out of elements that have no end,
And all confused at once, I understand,
Is not what makes a man to live forever.
O no, not now! He'll not be going now:
There'll be time yet for God knows what explosions   370
Before he goes. He'll stay awhile. Just wait:
Just wait a year or two for Cleopatra,
For she's to be a balsam° and a comfort;   something that soothes
And that's not all a jape° of mine now, either.   joke
For granted once the old way of Apollo   375
Sings in a man, he may then, if he's able,
Strike unafraid whatever strings he will
Upon the last and wildest of new lyres;°   stringed instruments
Nor out of his new magic, though it hymn
The shrieks of dungeoned hell, shall he create   380
A madness or a gloom to shut quite out
A cleaving daylight, and a last great calm
Triumphant over shipwreck and all storms..
He might have given Aristotle creeps,
But surely would have given him his *katharsis*.[13]   385

He'll not be going yet. There's too much yet
Unsung within the man. But when he goes,
I'd stake ye coin o' the realm his only care
For a phantom world he sounded° and found wanting   investigated
Will be a portion here, a portion there,   390
Of this or that thing or some other thing
That has a patent° and intrinsical°   clear; essential
Equivalence in those egregious° shillings.   wonderful
And yet he knows, God help him! Tell me, now,
If ever there was anything let loose   395

---

[13] *katharsis*. Aristotle used this word in the *Poetics* to describe the spiritual cleansing
    of great tragedy.

On earth by gods or devils heretofore
Like this mad, careful, proud, indifferent Shakespeare!
Where was it, if it ever was? By heaven,
'Twas never yet in Rhodes or Pergamon—
In Thebes or Nineveh, a thing like this!   400
No thing like this was ever out of England;
And that he knows. I wonder if he cares.
Perhaps he does. . . . O Lord, that House in Stratford!

1. Identify the *I* and the *you* in line 1. Where are they and what is the reason for their being together? Who is "our discriminate friend" mentioned in line 20?
2. What were Shakespeare's ambitions as the poet revealed them? What reasons are suggested for his inability to achieve his ambitions? What does the "House in Stratford" symbolize?
3. What kind of boy was Shakespeare? What kind of man was he when he first came to London? What was his attitude toward women?
4. What evidence is given in the poem that Shakespeare was "all at odds with all the unities"? What is revealed about his attitude toward life in his analogy of the spider and the fly?
5. About what ideas did Jonson disagree with Shakespeare? Despite their differences, why did Jonson say, "I love the man this side idolatry"?

Edna St. Vincent Millay

While still a student at Vassar, Edna Millay began to write poetry of intense, personal perception. In the anguish and intensity of her private emotions she found an absorbing reality to explore, to articulate, and to arrange in some kind of pattern. Her poems spoke to a whole generation of young people of the post-World War I era, young people who were aching for meaningful emotion to fill their emptiness. This emptiness resulted from the shattering of old established values and from the disillusionment of the peace which was no peace.

Miss Millay's singing lyricism gave new life to traditional forms and poetic techniques. Her poems are as charged with emotion as those of Emily Dickinson but are not as restrained and fanciful. They convey a deep absorption in the present situation, however fleeting, yet in many of her poems there is a longing for permanence such as may be found in the stability of nature or the lost simplicity of youth.

The Unexplorer

There was a road ran past our house
Too lovely to explore.
I asked my mother once—she said
That if you followed where it led
It brought you to the milk-man's door.   5
(That's why I have not traveled more.)

Describe the experience recounted in the poem. What led the poet to the conclusion expressed in line 6? What effect is gained by the offhand understatement that characterizes the poem? Is the tone of the poem suited to the thought?

Northern April

O mind, beset by music never for a moment quiet,—
The wind at the flue, the wind strumming the shutter;
The soft, antiphonal speech of the doubled brook,
      never for a moment quiet;
The rush of the rain against the glass, his voice in the
      eaves-gutter!

Where shall I lay you to sleep, and the robins be quiet?   5
Lay you to sleep—and the frogs be silent in the marsh?
Crashes the sleet from the bough and the bough sighs upward,
      never for a moment quiet.
April is upon us, pitiless and young and harsh.

O April, full of blood, full of breath, have pity upon us!
Pale, where the winter like a stone has been lifted away,
      we emerge like yellow grass.   10
Be for a moment quiet, buffet us not, have pity upon us,
Till the green come back into the vein, till the
      giddiness pass.

1. Why do you think the poet asked April to "have pity upon us"?
   To whom was she speaking in stanzas 1 and 2 and in stanza 3? What
   comparison was she suggesting between our feelings in April and the
   changes in nature at this time? Note the metaphor "the green come
   back into the vein" (line 12) and the last simile in line 10.

2. What evidence did the poet give in stanzas 1 and 2 to support her
   statement in line 8? As you examine the sensory impressions in these
   stanzas, indicate what they have in common.

3. Discuss the effect of the exclamatory nature of stanza 1 and the
   rhetorical questions (lines 5 and 6) on the meaning and mood of
   the poem. Discuss also the effect of the alliteration, the rhythm, the
   combination of long and short lines, and the repetition of certain
   words and phrases.

4. In writing about spring, some poets rely on "pretty" adjectives to convey their impressions. Show how Miss Millay's choice of language has made this poem lively and vigorous.

Pity Me Not Because the Light of Day

Pity me not because the light of day
At close of day no longer walks the sky;
Pity me not for beauties passed away
From field and thicket as the year goes by;
Pity me not the waning of the moon,   5
Nor that the ebbing tide goes out to sea,
Nor that a man's desire is hushed so soon,
And you no longer look with love on me.

This have I known always: love is no more
Than the wide blossom which the wind assails;   10
Than the great tide that treads the shifting shore,
Strewing fresh wreckage gathered in the gales.
Pity me that the heart is slow to learn
What the swift mind beholds at every turn.

[handwritten annotations: A sonnet is a poem with 14 lines / A Shakespeare sonnet / 8 lines 6 lines / Last 2 lines in heroic couplet / 2 lines that rhyme / She was sorry that her heart didn't learn what her mind knew / blossom falls apart]

1. What had the poet known always? What had she come to accept "as the year goes by" and for which she asked no pity? For what *did* she ask pity? Give your interpretation of the last two lines of the poem.

2. Point out the images in lines 9-12 and indicate what you think they reveal about the nature of love.

3. What evidence (rhythm pattern and rhyme scheme) indicates that this poem is a Shakespearean sonnet? Point out the way in which the sonnet form is related to the development of the ideas in the poem.

4. Miss Millay's choice of the "exact word" was as important to the sound of the poem as to the images created in the mind. Note, for example, the *m* and *n* sounds in line 5. Point out examples of alliteration and assonance which impressed you and tell why.

I Shall Go Back Again

I shall go back again to the bleak shore
And build a little shanty on the sand
In such a way that the extremest band
Of brittle seaweed will escape my door
But by a yard or two, and nevermore   5
Shall I return to take you by the hand;
I shall be gone to what I understand
And happier than I ever was before.

The love that stood a moment in your eyes,
The words that lay a moment on your tongue,   10
Are one with all that in a moment dies,
A little under-said and over-sung;
But I shall find the sullen rocks and skies
Unchanged from what they were when I was young.

1. Why did the poet believe that by going back she would be happier
   than she ever was before? In line 7 she implied that she was leaving
   behind what she did not understand. What do you think it was?

2. What kind of things was she seeking by going back to what she had
   once known? What clues in the poem suggest that the happiness she
   expected to find would, or would not, last?

3. What reason can you see for the poet's describing the rocks and the
   skies as sullen? What contrast did she express in lines 9-12 between
   love and the rocks and skies?

Love, Though for This You Riddle Me with Darts

Love, though for this you riddle me with darts,
And drag me at your chariot till I die,—
Oh, heavy prince! Oh, panderer° of hearts!—   go-between
Yet hear me tell how in their throats they lie
Who shout you mighty: thick about my hair,   5
Day in, day out, your ominous arrows purr,
Who still am free, unto no querulous° care   fretful
A fool, and in no temple worshiper!
I, that have bared me to your quiver's fire,
Lifted my face into its puny rain,   10
Do wreathe° you Impotent to Evoke Desire   crown
As you are Powerless to Elicit Pain!
(Now will the god, for blasphemy so brave,
Punish me, surely, with the shaft I crave!)

1. What is the attitude of the speaker in the poem toward the god who has riddled her with darts? Who is this god? Why did she call him Impotent and Powerless? What reason can you give for capitalizing these and other words in lines 11 and 12?

2. Give your interpretation of the last two lines, particularly the phrase "with the shaft I crave." Do these lines express an attitude different from that expressed in the preceding lines? If so, which is the poet's real attitude?

3. Why is the god referred to as "heavy prince" and "panderer of hearts"? To whom does who refer in line 5? Is who in line 7 the same person or a different one?

4. Point out the images used to picture the assault of the god's weapon and its effect. Note the rhyming of line 6 and line 8. Is this a faulty rhyme? Explain why or why not.

God's World

O World, I cannot hold thee close enough!
  Thy winds, thy wide grey skies!
  Thy mists, that roll and rise!
Thy woods, this autumn day, that ache and sag
And all but cry with color! That gaunt crag   5
To crush! To lift the lean of that black bluff!
World, World, I cannot get thee close enough!

Long have I known a glory in it all,
  But never knew I this;
  Here such a passion is   10
As stretcheth me apart. Lord, I do fear
Thou'st made the world too beautiful this year.
My soul is all but out of me,—let fall
No burning leaf; prithee, let no bird call.

1. As the poet looked about her at God's world, what were her emotions? How do you interpret the first and last lines of stanza 1?

2. What led the poet to say, "My soul is all but out of me"? What request did she make? What did she fear?

3. Compare the emotions conveyed in stanzas 1 and 2. How are they the same or different? Find evidence in the poem to support your opinion.

4. Note the word *glory* in line 8. What reaction to the beauty of autumn does it suggest? In line 9, to what does *this* refer?

5. This poem is unusual in a number of ways; for example, the seven-line stanza, the short-line couplet (lines 2 and 3 and 9 and 10), and the rhyme scheme. Discuss each of these and the effect you think it has on the meaning and emotion of the poem.

Song of a Second April

April this year, not otherwise
  Than April of a year ago,
Is full of whispers, full of sighs,
  Of dazzling mud and dingy snow;
  Hepaticas that pleased you so   5
Are here again, and butterflies.

There rings a hammering all day,
  And shingles lie about the doors;
In orchards near and far away
  The grey wood-pecker taps and bores;   10
  And men are merry at their chores,
And children earnest at their play.

The larger streams run still and deep,
  Noisy and swift the small brooks run;
Among the mullein stalks the sheep   15
  Go up the hillside in the sun,
  Pensively,—only you are gone,
You that alone I cared to keep.

1. To whom is this poem addressed? Why is the word *second* in the title important? What mood is created in the poem?

2. What effect does the simple language have on the emotion conveyed in the poem? What is this emotion? In what respects is it affected by the description of the house, the workmen, the children, and the sheep?

3. Plot the meter and rhyme scheme of stanza 3. What is the predominant foot? What effect is achieved by the use of a different foot at the beginning of lines 14 and 17? What effect is achieved by the slight imperfection of the rhyme in line 17? What is added to the effect by picking up the sound of *gone* in the word *alone* (line 18)?

Renascence

This poem about a personal mystical experience was written when
Miss Millay was still in high school.

All I could see from where I stood
Was three long mountains and a wood;
I turned and looked another way,
And saw three islands in a bay.
So with my eyes I traced the line   5
Of the horizon, thin and fine,
Straight around till I was come
Back to where I'd started from;
And all I saw from where I stood
Was three long mountains and a wood.   10
Over these things I could not see;
These were the things that bounded me;
And I could touch them with my hand,
Almost, I thought, from where I stand.
And all at once things seemed so small   15
My breath came short, and scarce at all.
But, sure, the sky is big, I said;
Miles and miles above my head;
So here upon my back I'll lie
And look my fill into the sky.   20
And so I looked, and, after all,
The sky was not so very tall.
The sky, I said, must somewhere stop,
And—sure enough!—I see the top!
The sky, I thought, is not so grand;   25
I 'most could touch it with my hand!
And, reaching up my hand to try,
I screamed to feel it touch the sky.

I screamed, and—lo!—Infinity
Came down and settled over me;   30

Forced back my scream into my chest,
Bent back my arm upon my breast,
And, pressing of the Undefined
The definition on my mind,
Held up before my eyes a glass   35
Through which my shrinking sight did pass
Until it seemed I must behold
Immensity made manifold;
Whispered to me a word whose sound
Deafened the air for worlds around,   40
And brought unmuffled to my ears
The gossiping of friendly spheres,
The creaking of the tented sky,
The ticking of Eternity.

I saw and heard, and knew at last   45
The How and Why of all things, past,
And present, and forevermore.
The universe, cleft to the core,
Lay open to my probing sense
That, sickening, I would fain pluck thence   50
But could not,—nay! But needs must suck
At the great wound, and could not pluck
My lips away till I had drawn
All venom out.—Ah, fearful pawn!
For my omniscience I paid toll   55
In infinite remorse of soul.
All sin was of my sinning, all
Atoning mine, and mine the gall
Of all regret. Mine was the weight
Of every brooded wrong, the hate   60
That stood behind each envious thrust,
Mine every greed, mine every lust.
And all the while for every grief,
Each suffering, I craved relief
With individual desire,—   65
Craved all in vain! And felt fierce fire
About a thousand people crawl;
Perished with each,—then mourned for all!
A man was starving in Capri;

He moved his eyes and looked at me;   70
I felt his gaze, I heard his moan,
And knew his hunger as my own.
I saw at sea a great fog-bank
Between two ships that struck and sank;
A thousand screams the heavens smote;   75
And every scream tore through my throat;
No hurt I did not feel, no death
That was not mine; mine each last breath
That, crying, met an answering cry
From the compassion that was I.   80
All suffering mine, and mine its rod;
Mine, pity like the pity of God.
Ah, awful weight! Infinity
Pressed down upon the finite me!
My anguished spirit, like a bird,   85
Beating against my lips I heard;
Yet lay the weight so close about
There was no room for it without.
And so beneath the weight lay I
And suffered death, but could not die.   90

Long had I lain thus, craving death,
When quietly the earth beneath
Gave way, and inch by inch, so great
At last had grown the crushing weight,
Into the earth I sank till I   95
Full six feet under ground did lie,
And sank no more,—there is no weight
Can follow here, however great.
From off my breast I felt it roll,
And as it went my tortured soul   100
Burst forth and fled in such a gust
That all about me swirled the dust.

Deep in the earth I rested now;
Cool is its hand upon the brow
And soft its breast beneath the head   105
Of one who is so gladly dead.

And all at once, and over all,
The pitying rain began to fall.
I lay and heard each pattering hoof
Upon my lowly, thatchèd roof.   110
And seemed to love the sound far more
Than ever I had done before.
For rain it hath a friendly sound
To one who's six feet underground;
And scarce the friendly voice or face: 115
A grave is such a quiet place.

The rain, I said, is kind to come
And speak to me in my new home.
I would I were alive again
To kiss the fingers of the rain,   120
To drink into my eyes the shine
Of every slanting silver line,
To catch the freshened, fragrant breeze
From drenched and dripping apple-trees.
For soon the shower will be done,   125
And then the broad face of the sun
Will laugh above the rain-soaked earth
Until the world with answering mirth
Shakes joyously, and each round drop
Rolls, twinkling, from its grass-blade top.   130
How can I bear it; buried here,
While overhead the sky grows clear
And blue again after the storm?
O, multi-colored, multiform,
Belovèd beauty over me,   135
That I shall never, never see
Again! Spring-silver, autumn-gold,
That I shall never more behold!
Sleeping your myriad magics through,
Close-sepulchered away from you!   140
O God, I cried, give me new birth,
And put me back upon the earth!
Upset each cloud's gigantic gourd
And let the heavy rain, down-poured

In one big torrent, set me free,   145
Washing my grave away from me!

I ceased; and, through the breathless hush
That answered me, the far-off rush
Of herald wings came whispering
Like music down the vibrant string   150
Of my ascending prayer, and—crash!
Before the wild wind's whistling lash
The startled storm-clouds reared on high
And plunged in terror down the sky,
And the big rain in one black wave   155
Fell from the sky and struck my grave.

I know not how such things can be,
I only know there came to me
A fragrance such as never clings
To aught save happy living things;   160
A sound as of some joyous elf
Singing sweet songs to please himself,
And, through and over everything,
A sense of glad awakening.
The grass, a tip-toe at my ear,   165
Whispering to me I could hear;
I felt the rain's cool finger-tips
Brushed tenderly across my lips,
Laid gently on my sealèd sight,
And all at once the heavy night   170
Fell from my eyes and I could see,—
A drenched and dripping apple-tree,
A last long line of silver rain,
A sky grown clear and blue again.
And as I looked a quickening gust   175
Of wind blew up to me and thrust
Into my face a miracle
Of orchard-breath, and with the smell,—
I know not how such things can be!—
I breathed my soul back into me.   180

Ah! Up then from the ground sprang I
And hailed the earth with such a cry

As is not heard save from a man
Who has been dead and lives again.
About the trees my arms I wound;   185
Like one gone mad I hugged the ground;
I raised my quivering arms on high;
I laughed and laughed into the sky,
Till at my throat a strangling sob
Caught fiercely, and a great heart-throb   190
Sent instant tears into my eyes;
O God, I cried, no dark disguise
Can e'er hereafter hide from me
Thy radiant identity!
Thou canst not move across the grass   195
But my quick eyes will see Thee pass,
Nor speak, however silently,
But my hushed voice will answer Thee.
I know the path that tells Thy way
Through the cool eve of every day;   200
God, I can push the grass apart
And lay my finger on Thy heart!

The world stands out on either side
No wider than the heart is wide;
Above the world is stretched the sky,—   205
No higher than the soul is high.
The heart can push the sea and land
Farther away on either hand;
The soul can split the sky in two,
And let the face of God shine through.   210
But East and West will pinch the heart
That cannot keep them pushed apart;
And he whose soul is flat—the sky
Will cave in on him by and by.

1. The word *renascence* means "rebirth" or "revival." Why is it an appropriate title for this poem?
2. What made the poet's breath come short? What was there about the physical setting (lines 1-28) that led to the first steps in her mystical experience? What feeling led up to the poet's scream?

3. What new kind of awareness did the poet experience (lines 29-53)? What toll did she pay for her omniscience? What did she mean in line 90?

4. Describe what happened to the poet (lines 91-116) and what change occurred in her emotions. What restored her desire to be alive again? How was her prayer answered?

5. What effect did her rebirth have on her? What new knowledge did she acquire by the experience?

6. Identify the predominant rhythm pattern of the poem. Is it highly regular throughout? Discuss the way in which the poet avoided monotony in a long poem despite regular rhythm and couplet rhyming. What effect is produced by the frequent alliteration?

Elegy

This is the fifth in a series of poems Miss Millay wrote in memory of a college friend who died soon after her graduation from Vassar.

Let them bury your big eyes
In the secret earth securely,
Your thin fingers, and your fair,
Soft, indefinite-colored hair,—
All of these in some way, surely, 5
From the secret earth shall rise.
Not for these I sit and stare,
Broken and bereft completely;
Your young flesh that sat so neatly
On your little bones will sweetly 10
Blossom in the air.

But your voice,—never the rushing
Of a river underground,
Not the rising of the wind
In the trees before the rain, 15
Not the woodcock's watery call,
Not the note the white-throat utters,

Not the feet of children pushing
Yellow leaves along the gutters
In the blue and bitter fall,   20
Shall content my musing mind
For the beauty of that sound
That in no new way at all
Ever will be heard again.

Sweetly through the sappy stalk   25
Of the vigorous weed,
Holding all it held before,
Cherished by the faithful sun,
On and on eternally
Shall your altered fluid run,   30
Bud and bloom and go to seed;
But your singing days are done;
But the music of your talk
Never shall the chemistry
Of the secret earth restore.   35
All your lovely words are spoken.
Once the ivory box is broken,
Beats the golden bird no more.

1. What reassurance did the poet find that softened her grief? What
   did she miss most of all? Where would she look for it and not find it?
   Why was it gone forever?

2. Note the metaphors in lines 37 and 38. To what do the ivory box
   and the golden bird refer? Express in your own words the over-all idea
   or theme of the poem as summarized in the last stanza and particularly
   in the last two lines.

3. Look again at the images in stanza 1. Which are expanded in lines
   32-36? In your opinion, do these expansions increase or decrease the
   effectiveness of the poem? Explain.

4. Plot the rhyme scheme of the poem. What reason can you see for
   changing the rhyme scheme from stanza to stanza? What is the predominant rhythm pattern? What metrical foot occurs most frequently?
   Note the lines in which the poet has varied the meter, particularly
   at the beginning of lines. What is the effect of this variation?

Robert Frost

There is little doubt that Robert Frost is the best known and best loved of modern American poets. The wide range of his mind, his love of human beings and human experience, and his straightforwardness have won him a devoted following. Though his temperament and language were deeply grounded in northern New England, Frost was no narrow regional poet. He spoke to Americans everywhere, and in the language of their heritage, of man's relation to a rich but relentless land. In the many moods of nature he saw reflected man's own changing and vital moods.

Frost's poems reveal a calm detachment tinged with a wise philosophic acceptance. They are not, however, lacking in emotion. The growth of his wisdom through the years has given his verse an increasing depth and range. The form in which Frost spoke is traditional, but the voice was distinctly his own.

Reluctance

Out through the fields and the woods
   And over the walls I have wended;
I have climbed the hills of view
   And looked at the world, and descended;
I have come by the highway home,   5
   And lo, it is ended.

The leaves are all dead on the ground,
   Save those that the oak is keeping
To ravel them one by one

And let them go scraping and creeping   10
Out over the crusted snow,
   When others are sleeping.

And the dead leaves lie huddled and still,
   No longer blown hither and thither;
The last lone aster is gone;   15
   The flowers of the witch-hazel wither;
The heart is still aching to seek,
   But the feet question "Whither?"

Ah, when to the heart of man
   Was it ever less than a treason   20
To go with the drift of things,
   To yield with a grace to reason,
And bow and accept the end
   Of a love or a season?

1. The key to the mood and the meaning of the poem is suggested in the title. What had the poet seen on his walk that led him to ask the question expressed in stanza 4? How do you interpret lines 17 and 18?
2. What mood is created in the first three stanzas? What line best expresses the intensity of this mood?
3. In stanza 4, what did the poet consider a treason to the heart of man? What reason, or reasons, can you give for his attitude?
4. This poem appeared in *A Boy's Will*, Frost's first volume of poems. Do you think he would, or would not, express today the same reluctance to accept the end of things he cherished? Discuss.
5. Stanza 2 presents a detailed picture of the way the oak tree drops its leaves. What significance does this picture have for the meaning of the poem? Relate the various details of the description to the meaning.
6. Note the length and rhythm of the last line of each stanza. Compare it with the predominant rhythm of the other lines. What is the effect of these last lines?

Into My Own

One of my wishes is that those dark trees,
So old and firm they scarcely show the breeze,
Were not, as 'twere, the merest mask of gloom,
But stretched away unto the edge of doom.

I should not be withheld but that some day   5
Into their vastness I should steal away,
Fearless of ever finding open land,
Or highway where the slow wheel pours the sand.

I do not see why I should e'er turn back,
Or those should not set forth upon my track   10
To overtake me, who should miss me here
And long to know if still I held them dear.

They would not find me changed from him they knew—
Only more sure of all I thought was true.

1. On the surface this poem is about a dark forest and a journey. What
    does each symbolize? What clue do you find in the title? Which lines
    and words in stanza 1 give you an idea of what the forest symbolizes?
    In stanza 2 what do you think that the open land and the highway
    stand for? Why do you think the journey would leave the poet
    unchanged yet more sure (lines 13-14)? In the last line, to what does
    all refer?
2. Note that the poem is composed of a series of couplets. What reason
    can you see for their being arranged in stanzas? What is the predomi-
    nant rhythm pattern? What is the effect of the change of rhythm in
    line 8? What accounts for this change?

A Prayer in Spring

Oh, give us pleasure in the flowers to-day;
And give us not to think so far away
As the uncertain harvest; keep us here
All simply in the springing of the year.

Oh, give us pleasure in the orchard white,   5
Like nothing else by day, like ghosts by night;
And make us happy in the happy bees,
The swarm dilating round the perfect trees.

And make us happy in the darting bird
That suddenly above the bees is heard,   10
The meteor that thrusts in with needle bill,
And off a blossom in mid air stands still.

For this is love and nothing else is love,
The which it is reserved for God above
To sanctify to what far ends He will,   15
But which it only needs that we fulfil.

1. Why is this poem called "A Prayer in Spring"? Point out ways in which the language conveys the mood of a prayer. What attitude of mind did the poet pray for? In lines 2 and 3 what did he suggest might destroy this attitude?

2. In line 13, what does *this* refer to? Explain the meaning of lines 14, 15, 16.

3. What kind of bird is the "darting bird"? What phrases help you to visualize and identify the bird? What is the meaning of the word *dilating* as used in line 8? What pictures does it bring to mind?

4. Chart the rhythm pattern and identify the metrical line and foot. In what lines in stanza 3 does the sense demand a stress different from that of the dominant meter? What effect does this give to the stanza?

The Tuft of Flowers

I went to turn the grass after one
Who mowed it in the dew before the sun.

The dew was gone that made his blade so keen
Before I came to view the levelled scene.

I looked for him behind an isle of trees;   5
I listened for his whetstone° on the breeze.   sharpening stone

But he had gone his way, the grass all mown,
And I must be, as he had been,—alone,

"As all must be," I said within my heart,
"Whether they work together or apart."   10

But as I said it, swift there passed me by
On noiseless wing a bewildered butterfly,

Seeking with memories grown dim o'er night
Some resting flower of yesterday's delight.

And once I marked his flight go round and round,   15
As where some flower lay withering on the ground.

And then he flew as far as eye could see,
And then on tremulous wing came back to me.

I thought of questions that have no reply,
And would have turned to toss the grass to dry;   20

But he turned first, and led my eye to look
At a tall tuft of flowers beside a brook,

A leaping tongue of bloom the scythe had spared
Beside a reedy brook the scythe had bared.

I left my place to know them by their name,   25
Finding them butterfly weed when I came.

The mower in the dew had loved them thus,
By leaving them to flourish, not for us,

Nor yet to draw one thought of ours to him,
But from sheer morning gladness at the brim.   30

The butterfly and I had lit upon,
Nevertheless, a message from the dawn,

That made me hear the wakening birds around,
And hear his long scythe whispering to the ground,

And feel a spirit kindred to my own;   35
So that henceforth I worked no more alone;

But glad with him, I worked as with his aid,
And weary, sought at noon with him the shade;

And dreaming, as it were, held brotherly speech
With one whose thought I had not hoped to reach.   40

"Men work together," I told him from the heart,
"Whether they work together or apart."

1. Why was the tuft of flowers "a message from the dawn"? In what
   ways was the mood of the poet changed by this message? What truth
   or observation about life did he convey through the experience he
   recounted? Express this truth or observation in your own words. Does
   this support or contradict his earlier observation (stanzas 4 and 5)?
   Explain.
2. Through the first 20 lines the poet created the picture of a farmer
   working alone as he turned the mowed hay to dry. What mood is

created in these lines? What details help to create it? What "questions
that have no reply" (line 19) do you think were going through the
poet's mind?

3. The effect of this poem (written in the language of everyday speech)
is heightened by the rhythm pattern and by occasional figures of speech
which sharpen the sensory impressions. Note, for example, "a leaping
tongue of bloom" (line 23). Find other examples.

In Hardwood Groves

The same leaves over and over again!
They fall from giving shade above
To make one texture of faded brown
And fit the earth like a leather glove.

Before the leaves can mount again   5
To fill the trees with another shade,
They must go down past things coming up
They must go down into the dark decayed.

They must be pierced by flowers and put
Beneath the feet of dancing flowers.   10
However it is in some other world
I know that this is the way in ours.

1. Robert Frost has always been a close observer of nature. What event
in nature is the subject of this poem? What general "rule of nature"
did he derive from this event? How did Frost feel about this "rule"?
Give your interpretation of his observation in the last two lines of the
poem.

2. Why do you think the word *must* in line 9 is italicized? In what way
can leaves "mount again to fill the trees with another shade"? In line
12, to what does *this* refer?

3. Give your interpretation of line 3. Then point out what is being compared in the simile in line 4. Tell why you do, or do not, consider the
simile appropriate and effective.

Mending Wall

Something there is that doesn't love a wall,
That sends the frozen-ground-swell under it,
And spills the upper boulders in the sun;
And makes gaps even two can pass abreast.
The work of hunters is another thing: 5
I have come after them and made repair
Where they have left not one stone on a stone,
But they would have the rabbit out of hiding,
To please the yelping dogs. The gaps I mean,
No one has seen them made or heard them made,   10
But at spring mending-time we find them there.
I let my neighbor know beyond the hill;
And on a day we meet to walk the line
And set the wall between us once again.
We keep the wall between us as we go.   15
To each the boulders that have fallen to each.
And some are loaves and some so nearly balls
We have to use a spell to make them balance:
'Stay where you are until our backs are turned!'
We wear our fingers rough with handling them.   20
Oh, just another kind of out-door game,
One on a side. It comes to little more:
There where it is we do not need the wall:
He is all pine and I am apple orchard.
My apple trees will never get across   25
And eat the cones under his pines, I tell him.
He only says, "Good fences make good neighbors."
Spring is the mischief in me, and I wonder
If I could put a notion in his head:
"Why do they make good neighbors? Isn't it   30
Where there are cows? But here there are no cows.
Before I built a wall I'd ask to know
What I was walling in or walling out,

And to whom I was like to give offence.
Something there is that doesn't love a wall,   35
That wants it down." I could say "Elves" to him,
But it's not elves exactly, and I'd rather
He said it for himself. I see him there
Bringing a stone grasped firmly by the top
In each hand, like an old-stone savage armed.   40
He moves in darkness as it seems to me,
Not of woods only and the shade of trees.
He will not go behind his father's saying,
And he likes having thought of it so well
He says again, "Good fences make good neighbors."   45

1. Do you think the purpose of this poem is to tell a story, as in a narrative poem, or to bring out some truth or observation about life and man? Explain.
2. What was Frost trying to make clear in lines 1-11? Why did he refer to the mending of the wall as "just another kind of out-door game"? Why didn't he consider it a necessary task? Did his neighbor think it was? How do you know?
3. What did Frost want his neighbor to say for himself (line 38)? Study lines 40-45. What kind of darkness did he suggest that his neighbor moved in? What relation can you see between the description of the neighbor and the neighbor's repeated statement: "Good fences make good neighbors"?
4. The idea or theme of this poem is suggested rather than stated. One clue might be the comparison in line 40; another, the reference to "darkness" in line 41. As you consider possible themes, see if you can find one that expresses Frost's concern throughout the poem.

Home Burial

He saw her from the bottom of the stairs
Before she saw him. She was starting down,
Looking back over her shoulder at some fear.
She took a doubtful step and then undid it
To raise herself and look again. He spoke   5

Advancing toward her: "What is it you see
From up there always—for I want to know."
She turned and sank upon her skirts at that,
And her face changed from terrified to dull.
He said to gain time: "What is it you see,"   10
Mounting until she cowered under him.
"I will find out now—you must tell me, dear."
She, in her place, refused him any help
With the least stiffening of her neck and silence.
She let him look, sure that he wouldn't see.   15
Blind creature; and a while he didn't see.
But at last he murmured, "Oh," and again, "Oh."

"What is it—what?" she said.

                    "Just that I see."

"You don't," she challenged. "Tell me what it is."   20

"The wonder is I didn't see at once.
I never noticed it from here before.
I must be wonted° to it—that's the reason.   accustomed
The little graveyard where my people are!
So small the window frames the whole of it.   25
Not so much larger than a bedroom, is it?
There are three stones of slate and one of marble,
Broad-shouldered little slabs there in the sunlight
On the sidehill. We haven't to mind those.
But I understand: it is not the stones,   30
But the child's mound—"

            "Don't, don't, don't, don't," she cried.

She withdrew shrinking from beneath his arm
That rested on the banister, and slid downstairs;
And turned on him with such a daunting° look,   intimidating 35
He said twice over before he knew himself:
"Can't a man speak of his own child he's lost?"

"Not you! Oh, where's my hat? Oh, I don't need it!

I must get out of here. I must get air.
I don't know rightly whether any man can."   40

"Amy! Don't go to someone else this time.
Listen to me. I won't come down the stairs."
He sat and fixed his chin between his fists.
"There's something I should like to ask you, dear."

"You don't know how to ask it."   45

                        "Help me, then."

Her fingers moved the latch for all reply.

"My words are nearly always an offence.
I don't know how to speak of anything
So as to please you. But I might be taught   50
I should suppose. I can't say I see how.
A man must partly give up being a man
With women-folk. We could have some arrangement
By which I'd bind myself to keep hands off
Anything special you're a-mind to name.   55
Though I don't like such things 'twixt those that love.
Two that don't love can't live together without them
But two that do can't live together with them."
She moved the latch a little. "Don't—don't go.
Don't carry it to someone else this time.   60
Tell me about it if it's something human.
Let me into your grief. I'm not so much
Unlike other folks as your standing there
Apart would make me out. Give me my chance.
I do think, though, you overdo it a little.   65
What was it brought you up to think it the thing
To take your mother-loss of a first child
So inconsolably—in the face of love.
You'd think his memory might be satisfied—"

"There you go sneering now!"   70

                    "I'm not, I'm not!
You make me angry. I'll come down to you.
God, what a woman! And it's come to this,
A man can't speak of his own child that's dead."

"You can't because you don't know how to speak.   75
If you had any feelings, you that dug
With your own hand—how could you?—his little grave;
I saw you from that very window there,
Making the gravel leap and leap in air,
Leap up, like that, like that, and land so lightly   80
And roll back down the mound beside the hole.
I thought, Who is that man? I didn't know you.
And I crept down the stairs and up the stairs
To look again, and still your spade kept lifting.
Then you came in. I heard your rumbling voice   85
Out in the kitchen, and I don't know why,
But I went near to see with my own eyes.
You could sit there with the stains on your shoes
Of the fresh earth from your own baby's grave
And talk about your everyday concerns.   90
You had stood the spade up against the wall
Outside there in the entry, for I saw it."

"I shall laugh the worst laugh I ever laughed.
I'm cursed. God, if I don't believe I'm cursed."

"I can repeat the very words you were saying.   95
'Three foggy mornings and one rainy day
Will rot the best birch fence a man can build.'
Think of it, talk like that at such a time!
What had how long it takes a birch to rot
To do with what was in the darkened parlor.   100
You *couldn't* care! The nearest friends can go
With anyone to death, comes so far short
They might as well not try to go at all.
No, from the time when one is sick to death,
One is alone, and he dies more alone.   105

Friends make pretence of following to the grave,
But before one is in it, their minds are turned
And making the best of their way back to life
And living people, and things they understand.
But the world's evil. I won't have grief so   110
If I can change it. Oh, I won't, I won't!"

"There, you have said it all and you feel better.
You won't go now. You're crying. Close the door.
The heart's gone out of it: why keep it up.
Amy! There's someone coming down the road!"   115

"You—oh, you think the talk is all. I must go—
Somewhere out of this house. How can I make you—"

"If—you—do!" She was opening the door wider.
"Where do you mean to go? First tell me that.
I'll follow and bring you back by force. I *will!*—"   120

1. What were the reasons for the wife's strange behavior and the estrange-
   ment between the wife and husband? Why did she believe that her
   husband was incapable of sharing her feelings?
2. In the husband's speech (lines 41-69) what is revealed about him and
   his feelings toward his wife?
3. What caused the husband's moods to shift during the conversation?
   Do you think he was justified?
4. What did the wife really resent (lines 101-111)? What did she really
   want to make her husband do or understand?
5. In lines 112-120 what is revealed about the basis of the conflict between
   the husband and wife?
6. In your opinion, what was the poet's attitude toward this human
   tragedy? What evidence can you find in the poem to support your
   opinion?
7. What insight does the poem provide into the difficulty of understanding another person's problems? What does the poem reveal about
   the way people usually behave when they cannot cope with this
   difficulty?
8. Point out how the poet has effectively used the elements of good
   story-telling in this poem; namely, plot, characterization, conflict, suspense, climax. In what ways is the use of dialogue especially effective?

9. Do you think the story which Frost told in verse would be as effective if told in prose? What is the effect of the compactness of poetry, the rhythm, the sound of the language? Point to specific sections of the poem to support your opinion. In your opinion, why did Frost leave the story "up in the air" at the end?

After Apple-Picking

My long two-pointed ladder's sticking through a tree
Toward heaven still,
And there's a barrel that I didn't fill
Beside it, and there may be two or three
Apples I didn't pick upon some bough.   5
But I am done with apple-picking now.
Essence of winter sleep is on the night,
The scent of apples: I am drowsing off.
I cannot rub the strangeness from my sight
I got from looking through a pane of glass   10
I skimmed this morning from the drinking trough
And held against the world of hoary° grass.   white with frost
It melted, and I let it fall and break.
But I was well
Upon my way to sleep before it fell,   15
And I could tell
What form my dreaming was about to take.
Magnified apples appear and disappear
Stem end and blossom end,
And every fleck of russet showing clear.   20
My instep arch not only keeps the ache,
It keeps the pressure of a ladder-round.
I feel the ladder sway as the boughs bend.
And I keep hearing from the cellar bin
The rumbling sound   25
Of load on load of apples coming in.
For I have had too much
Of apple-picking: I am overtired
Of the great harvest I myself desired.

There were ten thousand thousand fruit to touch,   30
Cherish in hand, lift down, and not let fall.
For all
That struck the earth,
No matter if not bruised or spiked with stubble,
Went surely to the cider-apple heap   35
As of no worth.
One can see what will trouble
This sleep of mine, whatever sleep it is.
Were he not gone,
The woodchuck could say whether it's like his   40
Long sleep, as I describe its coming on,
Or just some human sleep.

1. As the speaker in the poem thought about his apple harvest, what
   details did he recall most vividly? What likeness do you see between
   his recollection and the thoughts which pass through a person's mind
   just before he drops off to sleep? What is the poet's feeling about the
   harvest and about himself?

2. How do you account for the poet's many references to sleep? What
   did he mean by "essence of winter sleep" (line 7)? What relation can
   you see between the experience with the ice on the drinking trough
   (line 11) and the idea of sleep? What distinction did he make between
   the long sleep of the woodchuck (line 41) and "just some human
   sleep"?

3. Identify the predominant rhythm pattern, including the most frequently used metrical foot. How many feet are in most of the lines?
   What variations do you find? Are there any lines in which you have
   to force the accent in order to keep the rhythm pattern? Cite examples
   as evidence.

4. After you have charted the rhyme scheme of the poem, point out the
   ways in which it is unusual. What characteristics of colloquial speech
   do you find in the poem? On the basis of the rhythm pattern, the
   rhyme scheme, and the language, what similarity and difference can
   you see between this poem and the New England poems written a
   century ago?

Sand Dunes

Sea waves are green and wet,
But up from where they die,
Rise others vaster yet,
And those are brown and dry.

They are the sea made land   5
To come at the fisher town,
And bury in solid sand
The men she could not drown.

She may know cove and cape,
But she does not know mankind   10
If by any change of shape,
She hopes to cut off mind.

Men left her a ship to sink:
They can leave her a hut as well;
And be but more free to think   15
For the one more cast off shell.

1. What idea is expressed in the poem, particularly in the last stanza?
   To what does *she* refer? What did she hope to do? Why would her
   efforts end in failure? What did the poet reveal about her through his
   personification?
2. What picture did the poet create in stanzas 1 and 2? Where do the
   "green and wet waves" die? What are the "brown and dry waves"?
   Give your interpretation of stanza 2.
3. What does the "shell" in line 16 symbolize? What is the relation
   between the idea symbolized and the ship and the hut?

The Exposed Nest

You were forever finding some new play.
So when I saw you down on hands and knees
In the meadow, busy with the new-cut hay,
Trying, I thought, to set it up on end,
I went to show you how to make it stay,   5
If that was your idea, against the breeze,
And, if you asked me, even help pretend
To make it root again and grow afresh.
But 'twas no make-believe with you to-day,
Nor was the grass itself your real concern,   10
Though I found your hand full of wilted fern,
Steel-bright June-grass, and blackening heads of clover.
'Twas a nest full of young birds on the ground
The cutter-bar had just gone champing° over   biting and chewing
(Miraculously without tasting flesh)   15
And left defenseless to the heat and light.
You wanted to restore them to their right
Of something interposed between their sight
And too much world at once—could means be found.
The way the nest-full every time we stirred   20
Stood up to us as to a mother-bird
Whose coming home has been too long deferred,
Made me ask would the mother-bird return
And care for them in such a change of scene
And might our meddling make her more afraid.   25
That was a thing we could not wait to learn.
We saw the risk we took in doing good,
But dared not spare to do the best we could
Though harm should come of it; so built the screen
You had begun, and gave them back their shade.   30
All this to prove we cared. Why is there then
No more to tell? We turned to other things.

I haven't any memory—have you?—
Of ever coming to the place again
To see if the birds lived the first night through,   35
And so at last to learn to use their wings.

1. Who is the you in the poem? What is the relationship between the you and the poet? What had happened that they tried to remedy? What risk did they run? Why did they never learn the result of their caring?

2. Interpret the meaning of lines 27-29. How might this idea be applied to other situations in life?

3. Rewrite lines 17-26 in your own words and as a prose paragraph. Discuss the differences in word order, compactness, and rhythm between your prose paragraph and the lines of the poem.

4. Like many of Frost's poems, this one is rhymed, but not in a conventional way. To appreciate fully the poet's skill, you might chart the rhyme scheme to see how varied it is.

Dust of Snow

The way a crow
Shook down on me
The dust of snow
From a hemlock tree

Has given my heart   5
A change of mood
And saved some part
Of a day I had rued.°   regretted

1. In your opinion why did the incident described in stanza 1 produce "a change of mood" in the heart of the poet?

2. Note that the entire poem is a simple sentence. What effect is created by the simple structure, scant detail, and compactness?

On Looking Up By Chance at the Constellations

You'll wait a long, long time for anything much
To happen in heaven beyond the floats of cloud
And the Northern Lights that run like tingling nerves.
The sun and moon get crossed, but they never touch,
Nor strike out fire from each other, nor crash out loud.   5
The planets seem to interfere in their curves,
But nothing ever happens, no harm is done.
We may as well go patiently on with our life,
And look elsewhere than to stars and moon and sun
For the shocks and changes we need to keep us sane.   10
It is true the longest drouth will end in rain,
The longest peace in China will end in strife.
Still it wouldn't reward the watcher to stay awake
In hopes of seeing the calm of heaven break
On his particular time and personal sight.   15
That calm seems certainly safe to last tonight.

1. Why did the poet say "we may as well . . . look elsewhere than to
   stars and moon and sun for the shocks and changes"? Why does man
   need shocks and changes? What is the difference between the
   "changes" in lines 11 and 12 and those looked for in the heavens?
2. What did Frost imply about human nature in lines 13-15? The phrase
   "calm of heaven" has a figurative as well as a literal meaning. What is
   its figurative meaning? What is the relationship between the idea
   expressed in line 15 and the idea in line 8?
3. Note the tone of voice of the poet. Is it scolding, angry, bitter, sarcastic, melancholy, gay? You may prefer another adjective. What is
   there about the language and the relationship among the ideas which
   gives a clue to the tone?
4. How does the rhyme scheme in the last four lines differ from that in
   preceding lines? What reason can you see for the poet's changing the
   rhyme scheme at the end of the poem?

The Gift Outright

The land was ours before we were the land's.
She was our land more than a hundred years
Before we were her people. She was ours
In Massachusetts, in Virginia,
But we were England's, still colonials,   5
Possessing what we still were unpossessed by,
Possessed by what we now no more possessed.
Something we were withholding made us weak
Until we found it was ourselves
We were withholding from our land of living,   10
And forthwith found salvation in surrender.
Such as we were we gave ourselves outright
(The deed of gift was many deeds of war)
To the land vaguely realizing° westward,   coming into being
But still unstoried, artless, unenhanced,   15
Such as she was, such as she would become.

1. This is the poem that Robert Frost read at the inauguration of
   President Kennedy. What "gift outright" was he urging Americans
   to make? What relationship do you see between this gift and the
   following statement from the President's inaugural address: "Ask not
   what your country can do for you, but rather what you can do for your
   country"?
2. What period in American history was the poet examining in lines 1-7?
   Give your interpretation of these lines, particularly lines 6 and 7.
3. What was the "something" that made us, the colonials, weak? What
   did Frost mean by "our land of living" and "salvation in surrender"
   (lines 10 and 11)? In line 13, did he mean that the deeds of war were
   the gift or that they were the proof of the gift? How do you interpret
   this line?
4. In the last three lines, Frost referred to the years following our "salvation in surrender." To what does she refer? What challenge to
   Americans is expressed in these lines?

At Woodward's Gardens

A boy, presuming on his intellect,
Once showed two little monkeys in a cage
A burning-glass they could not understand
And never could be made to understand.
Words are no good: to say it was a lens   5
For gathering solar rays would not have helped.
But let him show them how the weapon worked.
He made the sun a pin-point on the nose
Of first one then the other till it brought
A look of puzzled dimness to their eyes   10
That blinking could not seem to blink away.
They stood arms laced together at the bars,
And exchanged troubled glances over life.
One put a thoughtful hand up to his nose
As if reminded—or as if perhaps   15
Within a million years of an idea.
He got his purple little knuckles stung.
The already known had once more been confirmed
By psychological experiment,
And that were all the finding to announce   20
Had the boy not presumed too close and long.
There was a sudden flash of arm, a snatch,
And the glass was the monkeys' not the boy's.
Precipitately° they retired back cage   immediately
And instituted an investigation   25
On their part, though without the needed insight.
They bit the glass and listened for the flavor.
They broke the handle and the binding off it.
Then none the wiser, frankly gave it up,
And having hid it in their bedding straw   30
Against the day of prisoners' ennui,°   boredom
Came dryly forward to the bars again

To answer for themselves: Who said it mattered
What monkeys did or didn't understand?
They might not understand a burning-glass.   35
They might not understand the sun itself.
It's knowing what to do with things that counts.

1. How did the monkeys react to the boy's experiment? Why were "words no good" in making them understand? How did the monkeys' behavior after seizing the glass illustrate that they were "without the needed insight?"
2. What wry comment in the last line was the poet making on the boy's experiment with his magnifying glass? Explain how the first line of the poem anticipates this comment. In your opinion, was the poet using the fable of the monkeys and the boy to satirize human pretensions? If so, what pretensions was he holding up to ridicule?
3. What meaning did the poet intend by the word *dryly* in line 32? Who is asking the question in lines 33 and 34? What relationship can you see between the statements in lines 35-37 and the technical advances made during the last twenty-five years?

The White-Tailed Hornet

The white-tailed hornet lives in a balloon
That floats against the ceiling of the woodshed.
The exit he comes out at like a bullet
Is like the pupil of a pointed gun.
And having power to change his aim in flight,   5
He comes out more unerring than a bullet.
Verse could be written on the certainty
With which he penetrates my best defense
Of whirling hands and arms about the head
To stab me in the sneeze-nerve of a nostril.   10
Such is the instinct of it I allow.
Yet how about the insect certainly
That in the neighborhood of home and children

Is such an execrable° judge of motives   wretched
As not to recognize in me the exception   15
I like to think I am in everything—
One who would never hang above a bookcase
His Japanese crepe-paper globe for trophy?
He stung me first and stung me afterward.
He rolled me off the field head over heels,   20
And would not listen to my explanations.

That's when I went as visitor to his house.
As visitor at my house he is better.
Hawking for flies about the kitchen door,
In at one door perhaps and out another,   25
Trust him then not to put you in the wrong.
He won't misunderstand your freest movements.
Let him light on your skin unless you mind
So many prickly grappling feet at once.
He's after the domesticated fly   30
To feed his thumping° grubs as big as he is.   whopping
Here he is at his best, but even here—
I watched him where he swooped, he pounced, he struck;
But what he found he had was just a nailhead.
He struck a second time. Another nailhead.   35
"Those are just nailheads. Those are fastened down."
Then disconcerted and not unannoyed,
He stooped and struck a little huckleberry
The way a player curls around a football.
"Wrong shape, wrong color, and wrong scent," I said.   40
The huckleberry rolled him on his head.
At last it was a fly. He shot and missed;
And the fly circled round him in derision.
But for the fly he might have made me think
He had been at his poetry, comparing   45
Nailhead with fly and fly with huckleberry:
How like a fly, how very like a fly.
But the real fly he missed would never do;
The missed fly made me dangerously skeptic.

Won't this whole instinct matter bear revision?   50
Won't almost any theory bear revision?

To err is human, not to, animal.
Or so we pay the compliment to instinct,
Only too liberal of our compliment
That really takes away instead of gives.   55
Our worship, humor, conscientiousness
Went long since to the dogs under the table.
And served us right for having instituted
Downward comparisons. As long on earth
As our comparisons were stoutly upward   60
With gods and angels, we were men at least,
But little lower than the gods and angels.
But once comparisons were yielded downward,
Once we began to see our images
Reflected in the mud and even dust,   65
'Twas disillusion upon disillusion.
We were lost piecemeal to the animals,
Like people thrown out to delay the wolves.
Nothing but fallibility° was left us,   liability to err
And this day's work made even that seem doubtful.   70

1. Early in the poem the poet must give the reader a clue to the way he wants his poem "to be taken." What tone did Frost set in lines 1-10 by such whimsical figures of speech as, "the sneeze-nerve of a nostril" (line 10)? If he had been deadly serious in his intent, would he have used such figures of speech? Explain. Did he maintain the same tone throughout the poem? If not, at what lines in the poem did the tone change? Cite examples to support your answers.

2. Point out other ways in which Frost revealed his attitude toward the ideas he was exploring; for example, exaggeration, contradiction, shift from serious to comic, and mock elegance. Give examples of each of these.

3. In line 11 what does *it* refer to? To what instinct was he referring in line 11? Why was Frost convinced that the hornet was a poor judge of motives? How did the behavior of the hornet change when it entered the poet's house? What experience left the hornet "disconcerted and not unannoyed" (line 37)?

4. Describe the actions of the hornet that led the poet to think that the hornet "had been at his poetry." What was the poet's reaction when the hornet missed the fly? How do you interpret lines 47-49?

5. In stanza 3 Frost began to draw conclusions based on what he had recounted in stanzas 1 and 2. What did he start to think about as he pondered the actions of the hornet? What theory (line 52) did he think would bear revision? Why did he call his theory a downward comparison?

6. Because of this downward comparison between man and animal, what qualities of man "went long since to the dogs under the table"? What final conclusion did Frost express in the last two lines of the poem? Tell why you do, or do not, think that he meant the reader to take seriously his comments in the last stanza and his conclusion in the last lines.

Triple Bronze

The Infinite's being so wide
Is the reason the Powers provide
For inner defense my hide.
For next defense outside

I make myself this time   5
Of wood or granite or lime
A wall too hard for crime
Either to breach or climb.

Then a number of us agree
On a national boundary.   10
And that defense makes three
Between too much and me.

1. What defense have the Powers provided man? Who are those Powers? What reason was given for this defense? How does it differ from the other two? Against what is man (represented by the poet) defending himself? In your opinion is the poet suggesting that with these defenses man is safe? Or is he suggesting that man will have to find new defenses

each time he finds "too much" more than he can handle? Give reasons
for your answers.

2. Against what were the second and third defenses built? What reason
can you give for the poet's use of the word *bronze* to describe the triple
defense? What does *bronze* represent? What clue does the word give
you to the attitude of the poet toward his subject?

3. What is unusual about the rhythm pattern and rhyme scheme of this
poem? In what lines do you think that the poet was forced by the
rhythm and rhyme in his choice and arrangement of words?

Two Tramps in Mud Time

Out of the mud two strangers came
And caught me splitting wood in the yard.
And one of them put me off my aim
By hailing cheerily "Hit them hard!"
I knew pretty well why he dropped behind   5
And let the other go on a way.
I knew pretty well what he had in mind:
He wanted to take my job for pay.

Good blocks of beech it was I split,
As large around as the chopping block;   10
And every piece I squarely hit
Fell splinterless as a cloven rock.
The blows that a life of self-control
Spares to strike for the common good
That day, giving a loose to my soul,   15
I spent on the unimportant wood.

The sun was warm but the wind was chill.
You know how it is with an April day
When the sun is out and the wind is still,
You're one month on in the middle of May.   20

But if you so much as dare to speak,
A cloud comes over the sunlit arch,
A wind comes off a frozen peak,
And you're two months back in the middle of March.

A bluebird comes tenderly up to alight   25
And fronts the wind to unruffle a plume
His song so pitched as not to excite
A single flower as yet to bloom.
It is snowing a flake: and he half knew
Winter was only playing possum.   30
Except in color he isn't blue,
But he wouldn't advise a thing to blossom.

The water for which we may have to look
In summertime with a witching-wand,
In every wheelrut's now a brook,   35
In every print of a hoof a pond.
Be glad of water, but don't forget
The lurking frost in the earth beneath
That will steal forth after the sun is set
And show on the water its crystal teeth.   40

The time when most I loved my task
These two must make me love it more
By coming with what they came to ask.
You'd think I never had felt before
The weight of an ax-head poised aloft,   45
The grip on earth of outspread feet.
The life of muscles rocking soft
And smooth and moist in vernal heat.

Out of the woods two hulking tramps
(From sleeping God knows where last night,   50
But not long since in the lumber camps).
They thought all chopping was theirs of right.
Men of the woods and lumberjacks,
They judged me by their appropriate tool.

Except as a fellow handled an ax,   55
They had no way of knowing a fool.

Nothing on either side was said.
They knew they had but to stay their stay
And all their logic would fill my head:
As that I had no right to play   60
With what was another man's work for gain.
My right might be love but theirs was need.
And where the two exist in twain
Theirs was the better right—agreed.

But yield who will to their separation,   65
My object in living is to unite
My avocation and my vocation
As my two eyes make one in sight.
Only where love and need are one,
And the work is play for mortal stakes,   70
Is the deed ever really done
For Heaven and the future's sakes.

1. What satisfaction did the poet find in splitting wood (lines 13-16)?
   What else was there about the job that made the poet love it (stanzas
   3-6)? Why did the coming of the two tramps make him love his job
   more? In what way does the mood of spring (see stanzas 3-5) match
   the mood of the poet revealed in stanza 6?

2. The tramps said nothing, yet their logic filled the poet's head. What
   was their logic? What were the rights (1) of the lumberjacks and
   (2) of the poet? Under what circumstances did the poet agree that
   "theirs was the better right"?

3. In stanza 9 what is the poet's object? Why does he think this is more
   important than the rights expressed in stanza 8?

4. Contrast the sound of the words in stanza 2 with the sound of the
   words in stanza 3. Point out combinations and repetitions of vowel
   and consonant sounds that create this contrast. How do the sound
   and the sense complement each other in the two stanzas? Find lines
   in other stanzas where sound and sense combine effectively.

A Record Stride

In a Vermont bedroom closet
With a door of two broad boards
And for back wall a crumbling old chimney
(And that's what their toes are towards),

I have a pair of shoes standing,   5
Old rivals of sagging leather,
Who once kept surpassing each other,
But now live even together.

They listen for me in the bedroom
To ask me a thing or two   10
About who is too old to go walking,
With too much stress on the who.

I wet one last year at Montauk
For a hat I had to save.
The other I wet at the Cliff House   15
In an extra-vagant wave.

Two entirely different grandchildren
Got me into my double adventure.
But when they grow up and can read this
I hope they won't take it for censure.   20

I touch my tongue to the shoes now
And unless my sense is at fault,
On one I can taste Atlantic,
On the other Pacific, salt.

One foot in each great ocean   25
Is a record stride or stretch.

The authentic shoes it was made in
I should sell for what they would fetch.

But instead I proudly devote them
To my museum and muse;   30
So the thick-skins needn't act thin-skinned
About being past-active shoes.

And I ask all to try to forgive me
For being as over-elated
As if I had measured the country   35
And got the United States stated.

1. Why didn't the poet sell the pair of shoes for what they would fetch?
   To what was he referring in the title of the poem?
2. What is the tone of the poem? Show the relationship between this
   tone and the poet's extended personification of the old pair of shoes.
   What further evidences in the poem indicate the way in which Frost
   wanted this poem to be read?
3. Despite Frost's witty playfulness in the way he presents his ideas, the
   poem has its serious moments. What feeling about himself did Frost
   reveal in line 12? Show how this feeling was expressed in a different
   way in stanza 8. What does the last stanza reveal about the poet's
   feeling?
4. Frost's witty playfulness is revealed in his choice and use of words.
   Point out the puns in stanzas 8 and 9. Note the play on words in lines
   31 and 32. How do you interpret these lines? Note, too, the words
   museum and muse in line 30. To what do they refer? How do they
   add to the humor of the poem?

Susan Nacci

Elinor Wylie

At the time of Elinor Wylie's sudden death in 1928, Edmund Wilson, the literary critic, wrote a commemorative essay in which he described her as being "passionate but detached, all-wordly-wise and yet unworldly, generous without devotion, ruthless without spite, laughing with unbiased intelligence over the disasters of the hurt creature her spirit inhabited, and the mistress of a wonderful language in which accuracy, vigor and splendor seemed to require no study and no effort and in which it spoke simply of its own divine estate. . . ."

Miss Wylie's poems reveal many of these qualities to the careful reader. Most of her poems are a delight to read yet difficult to discuss because of their concentrated intensity and her playful imagination.

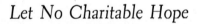

Let No Charitable Hope

Now let no charitable hope
Confuse my mind with images
Of eagle and of antelope:
I am in nature none of these.

I was, being human, born alone;   5
I am, being woman, hard beset;
I live by squeezing from a stone
The little nourishment I get.

In masks outrageous and austere
The years go by in single file;   10
But none has merited my fear,
And none has quite escaped my smile.

1. What did the images of the eagle and antelope suggest to the poet's mind? Why did she reject these images? Contrast what they represent with what she knew to be her true nature. What do lines 7 and 8 suggest about her life?
2. What impression of the passing years is suggested in lines 9 and 10? What was the poet's reaction to them?
3. Which phrases used by Edmund Wilson to describe the poet (page 68) most aptly apply to the person revealed in this poem?

Wild Peaches

1

When the world turns completely upside down
You say we'll emigrate to the Eastern Shore
Aboard a river-boat from Baltimore;
We'll live among wild peach trees, miles from town,
You'll wear a coonskin cap, and I a gown   5
Homespun, dyed butternut's dark gold color.
Lost, like your lotus-eating ancestor,
We'll swim in milk and honey till we drown.

The winter will be short, the summer long,
The autumn amber-hued, sunny and hot,   10
Tasting of cider and of scuppernong;°   wine grape
All seasons sweet, but autumn best of all.
The squirrels in their silver fur will fall
Like falling leaves, like fruit, before your shot.

2

The autumn frosts will lie upon the grass   15
Like bloom on grapes of purple-brown and gold.
The misted early mornings will be cold;
The little puddles will be roofed with glass.
The sun, which burns from copper into brass,
Melts these at noon, and makes the boys unfold   20
Their knitted mufflers; full as they can hold,
Fat pockets dribble chestnuts as they pass.

Peaches grow wild, and pigs can live in clover;
A barrel of salted herrings lasts a year;
The spring begins before the winter's over.   25
By February you may find the skins
Of garter snakes and water moccasins
Dwindled and harsh, dead-white and cloudy-clear.

3

When April pours the colors of a shell
Upon the hills, when every little creek   30
Is shot with silver from the Chesapeake
In shoals new-minted by the ocean swell,
When strawberries go begging, and the sleek
Blue plums lie open to the blackbird's beak,
We shall live well—we shall live very well.   35

The months between the cherries and the peaches
Are brimming cornucopias° which spill   horns of plenty
Fruits red and purple, somber-bloomed and black;
Then, down rich fields and frosty river beaches
We'll trample bright persimmons, while you kill   40
Bronze partridge, speckled quail, and canvasback.

4

Down to the Puritan marrow of my bones
There's something in this richness that I hate.
I love the look, austere, immaculate,
Of landscapes drawn in pearly monotones.   45
There's something in my very blood that owns
Bare hills, cold silver on a sky of slate,
A thread of water, churned to milky spate°   flood
Streaming through slanted pastures fenced with stones.

I love those skies, thin blue or snowy gray,   50
Those fields sparse-planted, rendering meager sheaves;
That spring, briefer than apple-blossom's breath,
Summer, so much too beautiful to stay,
Swift autumn, like a bonfire of leaves,
And sleepy winter, like the sleep of death.   55

1. Who are the you and *I* in the poem? What clues in stanza 1 tell you when and where they lived, and why the you proposed they emigrate? What kind of person do you think he was? What did the speaker mean in line 8?

2. What picture of the Eastern Shore is conveyed in Parts 1, 2, and 3? Where is this land of "milk and honey"? What evidence did she give to support the statement, "we shall live very well"?

3. In Part 4, why did the poet reject life on the Eastern Shore? What is the significance of the reference to *Puritan* in line 43? Compare the description of each season given in Part 4 with the description given in Parts 1, 2, and 3.

4. Point out examples of sensory images and figures of speech which you found most effective. Note particularly the poet's use of verbs in such images as "puddles *roofed* with glass," and "pockets *dribble* chestnuts." Find other images.

5. Chart the rhyme scheme of the poem, and then point out likenesses and differences among the stanzas and among the Parts. Tell why you do, or do not, think this scheme would be an easy one to manage. Point out those lines in which alliteration adds to the richness and effectiveness of the images.

The Eagle and the Mole

Avoid the reeking herd,
Shun the polluted flock,
Live like that stoic bird,
The eagle of the rock.

The huddled warmth of crowds   5
Begets and fosters hate;
He keeps, above the clouds,
His cliff inviolate.

When flocks are folded warm
And herds to shelter run,   10
He sails above the storm,
He stares into the sun.

If in the eagle's track
Your sinews cannot leap,
Avoid the lathered pack,   15
Turn from the steaming sheep.

If you would keep your soul
From spotted sight or sound,
Live like the velvet mole;
Go burrow underground.   20

And there hold intercourse
With roots of trees and stones,
With rivers at their source
And disembodied bones.

1. What does the eagle symbolize? Why does the poet refer to it as the "stoic bird"? (Consult a dictionary if you are not sure of the meaning of *stoic*.) What idea is suggested by *inviolate* (line 8)?

2. As the word *sheep* is applied to people, what qualities of character and behavior does it symbolize? For instance, what idea is suggested by the word *lathered* (line 15)? What words in stanzas 1-4 convey the poet's attitude toward such people? From what danger (stanza 5) does the soul need protection?

3. The way of life symbolized by the mole would seem to be just the opposite of that symbolized by the eagle. Why did the poet recommend it as an alternative choice? Is the tone of the poem serious or satirical? Base your answer on the poem and on the critic's comments quoted on page 68.

4. To whom is this poem directed? State in your own words the idea you think the poet meant to convey.

EXPERIMENTERS WITH FORM

AROUND the turn of the century, when the prose of photographic realism was still the vogue, there was a revival of interest in poetry, but in a kind that differed from that of the early New England poets. The new poets, particularly in the decade following 1910, made a conscious effort to explore new forms and techniques which would help them express themselves and their country. Whitman's loose, flowing free verse furnished a model which was developed in individual ways by such poets as Sandburg, Masters, Jeffers, and Williams. Not only did these poets free themselves from the traditional restrictions of form; they also revolutionized the generally accepted ideas regarding the subject matter of poetry. They believed that all aspects of modern life should be grist for the poet's mill.

Perhaps this new poetry evolved largely as a response to a new American way of life. People were moving in large numbers to the cities, which were becoming the centers of American life. The sprawling and energetic Midwest was replacing the conventionalized East as the dominant force in American culture. Thousands of foreigners emigrated to this country, bringing with them a diversity of language and culture which enriched it greatly. Industrialization led to a sense of restlessness and rootlessness, yet, at the same time, it freed men's minds from the traditional ways of life and thought.

In keeping with this change in American life, the center of poetic influence shifted from the Atlantic Coast to Chicago and to a group of expatriate Americans in Europe. With the publication of the small magazine, *Poetry*, there was little doubt that the new poetry, with its untraditional subject matter and new verse forms, was the beginning of a new tradition in poetic expression which was to equal, if not surpass, that of the first tradition which had won recognition nearly a century before.

The "New Poetry" derived much of its force from the prose realists. The new poets chose as their subject matter the real and contemporary, and as their language the speech of contemporary Americans. They discarded the traditional classical references and poetic diction which no longer appealed to their readers. Instead they turned to the forms and devices used by foreign poets whose work was then appearing in English translation. An even more important influence was a recognition of the pioneering work done by the four experimental poets of the preceding century. Whitman pointed the way to a greater freedom of verse form, to the use of everyday language, and to a broader interpretation of what is the subject matter of poetry. Poe and Lanier awakened the new poets to the evocative power of sound in words and rhythms. Emily Dickinson demonstrated the effect of sharp precision of image and dependence on concrete pictures or figures of speech in expressing the poet's special awareness of reality.

Vachel Lindsay

Vachel Lindsay spent much of his life wandering from town to town throughout America, performing his songs and selling his drawings in an effort to earn enough money for food and lodging. As he wandered, he listened to, and talked with, all kinds of people, gathering from them both the content of his verse and the form. No poet before him had succeeded so well in capturing the voices of America: the rhythm of evangelist preaching, the spontaneous singing of folk songs, the sounds of the highways he traveled, and the music of nature. He even included in his verse the rhythms of college cheering.

Lindsay's poetry was never intended to be read and analyzed by the lone reader at his desk. Some of his poems must be read aloud and listened to; some must be chanted by a group with a leader. Even his tender lyrics are better when shared.

Daniel

Darius the Mede was a king and a wonder.   *Beginning with a*
His eye was proud, and his voice was thunder.   *strain of "Dixie."*
He kept bad lions in a monstrous den.
He fed up the lions on Christian men.

Daniel was the chief hired man of the land.   *With a touch of*   5
He stirred up the jazz in the palace band.   *"Alexander's Ragtime*
He whitewashed the cellar. He shovelled in the coal.   *Band."*
And Daniel kept a-praying:—"Lord save my soul."
Daniel kept a-praying:—"Lord save my soul."
Daniel kept a-praying:—"Lord save my soul."   10

[75]

Daniel was the butler, swagger and swell.
He ran up stairs. He answered the bell.
And *he* would let in whoever came a-calling:—
Saints so holy, scamps so appalling.
"Old man Ahab leaves his card.   15
Elisha and the bears are a-waiting in the yard.
Here comes Pharaoh and his snakes a-calling.
Here comes Cain and his wife a-calling.
Shadrach, Meshach and Abednego for tea.
Here comes Jonah and the whale,   20
And the *Sea!*
Here comes St. Peter and his fishing pole.
Here comes Judas and his silver a-calling.
Here comes old Beelzebub a-calling."
And Daniel kept a-praying:—"Lord save my soul."   25
Daniel kept a-praying:—"Lord save my soul."
Daniel kept a-praying:—"Lord save my soul."

His sweetheart and his mother were Christian and meek.
They washed and ironed for Darius every week.
One Thursday he met them at the door:—   30
Paid them as usual, but acted sore.

He said:—"Your Daniel is a dead little pigeon.
He's a good hard worker, but he talks religion."
And he showed them Daniel in the lions' cage.
Daniel standing quietly, the lions in a rage.   35
His good old mother cried:—
"Lord save him."
And Daniel's tender sweetheart cried:—
"Lord save him."

And she was a golden lily in the dew.   *This to be repeated* 40
And she was as sweet as an apple on the tree *three times, very softly*
And she was as fine as a melon in the corn-field, *and slowly.*
Gliding and lovely as a ship on the sea,
Gliding and lovely as a ship on the sea.

And she prayed to the Lord:—   45
"Send Gabriel. Send Gabriel."

King Darius said to the lions:—
"Bite Daniel. Bite Daniel.
Bite him. Bite him. Bite him!"

Thus roared the lions:—   50
"We want Daniel, Daniel, Daniel,   *Here the audience roars*
We want Daniel, Daniel, Daniel.   *with the leader.*
Grrrrrrrrrrrrrrrrrrrrrrrrrrrrrrrrrrrrrrrrrrrrrr rrrrrrrrrrrrrrrrrrrrrrrr
Grrrrrrrrrrrrrrrrrrrrrrrrrrrrrrrrrrrrrrrrrrrrrrr rrrrrrrrrrrrrrrrrrrrrrrrr."

And Daniel did not frown,   55
Daniel did not cry.
He kept on looking at the sky.
And the Lord said to Gabriel:—
"Go chain the lions down,   *The audience sings this*
Go chain the lions down.   *with the leader, to the*
Go chain the lions down.   *old negro tune.*
Go chain the lions down."   60

And Gabriel chained the lions,
And Gabriel chained the lions,
And Gabriel chained the lions,   65
And Daniel got out of the den,
And Daniel got out of the den,
And Daniel got out of the den.
And Darius said:—"You're a Christian child,"
Darius said:—"You're a Christian child,"   70
Darius said:—"You're a Christian child,"
And gave him his job again,
And gave him his jog again,
And gave him his job again.

1. In what ways is this poem different from other poems in this book which were written by other authors?
2. Read this poem aloud in different ways, experimenting with changes of pitch, volume, and tempo. Note that each way creates a different effect. Tell why you think this kind of poem lends itself to various oral interpretations.
3. In stanza 6, which deals with Daniel's sweetheart, Lindsay suggested

in the margin that the phrase be repeated three times. Sometimes a
poet can overdo an effect. Tell why you think this repetition would,
or would not, spoil the total effect of the poem.

4. From what sources did the poet borrow material for both the content
and form of the poem?

5. Plot the rhythm pattern of the first two stanzas. In what lines did the
poet use strong beats? What effect do such lines have on the rhythmic
reading of the poem and on the impression the poet intended to
achieve?

Two Old Crows

Two old crows sat on a fence rail.
Two old crows sat on a fence rail,
Thinking of effect and cause,
Of weeds and flowers,
And nature's laws.   5
One of them muttered, one of them stuttered,
One of them stuttered, one of them muttered.
Each of them thought far more than he uttered.
One crow asked the other crow a riddle.
One crow asked the other crow a riddle: 10
The muttering crow
Asked the stuttering crow,
"Why does a bee have a sword to his fiddle?
Why does a bee have a sword to his fiddle?"
"Bee-cause," said the other crow,   15
"Bee-cause,
B B B B B B B B B B B B B B-cause."
Just then a bee flew close to their rail:—
"Buzzzzzzzzzz zzzzzzzzz   zzzzzzzz
        zzz zzzz zzzz zzzz   20
        ZZZZZZZZ."
And those two black crows
Turned pale,
And away those crows did sail.
Why?   25

B B B B B B B B B B B B B-cause.
B B B B B B B B B B B B B-cause.
"Buzzzzzzzzzz zzzzzzzz   zzzzzzzzz
    zzz zzzzzzzzzzzzzz
    ZZZZZZZZ."

1. This poem was obviously created for the fun of the sounds. As you read it aloud, try to convey the kinds of sounds suggested by the meaning and by the typography. How does the shape of the poem contribute to its effectiveness?
2. Note that the poet repeated some lines and inverted others. Explain as best you can why he did this and the effect you think he wanted to create.
3. In your opinion, what do the sword and the fiddle of the bee represent? What humor is gained by the poet's play on the meaning of the words? What would happen to the meaning if you pronounced *because* "bee-caws-zzz"?

Euclid

Old Euclid drew a circle
On a sand-beach long ago.
He bounded and enclosed it
With angles thus and so.
His set of solemn graybeards   5
Nodded and argued much
Of arc and of circumference,
Diameter and such.
A silent child stood by them
From morning until noon   10
Because they drew such charming
Round pictures of the moon.

Who was Euclid? What is revealed about the attitude of the poet by the words *solemn graybeards*? Why did the child see something different from what the graybeards saw? What two different ways of looking at the world are symbolized by the incident in the poem?

The Santa-Fé Trail (A Humoresque)

(I asked the old negro: "What is that bird that sings so well?"
He answered: "That is the Rachel-Jane." "Hasn't it another name
—lark, or thrush, or the like?" "No. Jus' Rachel-Jane.")

I. In Which a Racing Auto Comes from the East

This is the order of the music of the morning:— *To be sung delicately,*
                                                 to an improvised tune.
First, from the far East comes but a crooning.
The crooning turns to a sunrise singing.
Hark to the *calm*-horn, *balm*-horn, *psalm*-horn.
Hark to the *faint*-horn, *quaint*-horn, *saint*-horn 5

Hark to the *pace*-horn, *chase*-horn, *race*-horn. *To be sung or read*
                                                     with great speed.
And the holy veil of the dawn has gone.
Swiftly the brazen car comes on.
It burns in the East as the sunrise burns.
I see great flashes where the far trail turns.   10
Its eyes are lamps like the eyes of dragons.
It drinks gasoline from big red flagons.
Butting through the delicate mists of the morning,
It comes like lightning, goes past roaring.
It will hail all the windmills, taunting, ringing, 15
Dodge the cyclones,
Count the milestones,
On through the ranges the prairie-dog tills—
Scooting past the cattle on the thousand hills. ... 19
Ho for the *tear*-horn, *scare*-horn, *dare*-horn, *To be read or sung*
                                                    in a rolling bass,
                                         with some deliberation.
Ho for the *gay*-horn, *bark*-horn, *bay*-horn.
Ho for Kansas, land that restores us
When houses choke us, and great books bore us!
Sunrise Kansas, harvesters' Kansas,
A million men have found you before us.   25
A million men have found you before us.

II. In Which Many Autos Pass Westward

I want live things in their pride to remain.
In an even, deliberate, narrative manner.
I will not kill one grasshopper vain
Though he eats a hole in my shirt like a door.
I let him out, give him one chance more.   30
Perhaps, while he gnaws my hat in his whim,
Grasshopper lyrics occur to him.

I am a tramp by the long trail's border,
Given to squalor, rags and disorder.
I nap and amble and yawn and look,   35
Write fool-thoughts in my grubby book,
Recite to the children, explore at my ease,
Work when I work, beg when I please,
Give crank-drawings, that make folks stare
To the half-grown boys in the sunset glare,   40
And get me a place to sleep in the hay
At the end of a live-and-let-live day.

I find in the stubble of the new-cut weeds
A whisper and a feasting, all one needs:
The whisper of the strawberries, white and red   45
Here where the new-cut weeds lie dead.

But I would not walk all alone till I die
Without some life-drunk horns going by.
Up round this apple-earth they come
Blasting the whispers of the morning dumb:—   50
Cars in a plain realistic row.
And fair dreams fade
When the raw horns blow.

On each snapping pennant
A big black name:—   55
The careering city
Whence each car came.
They tour from Memphis, Atlanta, Savannah,
Like a train-caller in a Union Depot
Tallahassee and Texarkana.

They tour from St. Louis, Columbus, Manistee,   60
They tour from Peoria, Davenport, Kankakee.
Cars from Concord, Niagara, Boston,
Cars from Topeka, Emporia, and Austin.
Cars from Chicago, Hannibal, Cairo.
Cars from Alton, Oswego, Toledo.   65
Cars from Buffalo, Kokomo, Delphi,
Cars from Lodi, Carmi, Loami.
Ho for Kansas, land that restores us
When houses choke us, and great books bore us!
While I watch the highroad   70
And look at the sky,
While I watch the clouds in amazing grandeur
Roll their legions without rain
Over the blistering Kansas plain—
While I sit by the milestone   75
And watch the sky,
The United States
Goes by.

Listen to the iron-horns, ripping, racking.   *To be given very harshly,*
                                                with a snapping explosiveness.
Listen to the quack-horns, slack and clacking.   80
Way down the road, trilling like a toad,
Here comes the *dice*-horn, here comes the *vice*-horn,
Here comes the *snarl*-horn, *brawl*-horn, *lewd*-horn,
Followed by the *prude*-horn, bleak and squeaking:—
(Some of them from Kansas, some of them from Kansas.)   85
Here comes the *hod*-horn, *plod*-horn, *sod*-horn,
Nevermore-to-roam-horn, *loam*-horn, *home*-horn.
(Some of them from Kansas, some of them from Kansas.)
          Far away the Rachel-Jane   *To be read or sung,*
                                             well-nigh in a whisper.
          Not defeated by the horns   90
          Sings amid a hedge of thorns:—
          "Love and life,
          Eternal youth—
          Sweet, sweet, sweet, sweet,
          Dew and glory,   95
          Love and truth,
          Sweet, sweet, sweet, sweet."

WHILE SMOKE-BLACK FREIGHTS ON THE DOUBLE-TRACKED RAILROAD,
DRIVEN AS THOUGH BY THE FOUL FIEND'S OX-GOAD,   *Louder and louder,*
faster and faster.
SCREAMING TO THE WEST COAST, SCREAMING TO THE EAST,   100
CARRY OFF A HARVEST, BRING BACK A FEAST,
AND HARVESTING MACHINERY AND HARNESS FOR THE BEAST,
THE HAND-CARS WHIZ, AND RATTLE ON THE RAILS,
THE SUNLIGHT FLASHES ON THE TIN DINNER-PAILS.

And then, in an instant, ye modern men,   *In a rolling bass,*
with increasing deliberation.
Behold the procession once again,   106
Listen to the iron-horns, ripping, racking,   *With a snapping explosiveness.*
Listen to the wise-horn, desperate-to-advise horn,
Listen to the fast-horn, kill-horn, blast-horn. . . .

    Far away the Rachel-Jane   *To be sung or read*
well-nigh in a whisper.
    Not defeated by the horns   111
    Sings amid a hedge of thorns:—
    Love and life,
    Eternal youth,
    Sweet, sweet, sweet, sweet,   115
    Dew and glory,
    Love and truth.
    Sweet, sweet, sweet, sweet.

The mufflers open on a score of cars   *To be brawled in the*
beginning with a snapping
With wonderful thunder,   *explosiveness, ending in a*
languorous chant.
CRACK, CRACK, CRACK,   121
CRACK-CRACK, CRACK-CRACK,
CRACK, CRACK, CRACK,
Listen to the gold-horn . . .
Old-horn . . .   125
Cold-horn . . .
And all of the tunes, till the night comes down
On hay-stack, and ant-hill, and wind-bitten town.
Then far in the west, as in the beginning,   *To be sung to exactly*
the same whispered tune as
Dim in the distance, sweet in retreating,   *the first five lines.*
Hark to the faint-horn, quaint-horn, saint-horn, 131
Hark to the calm-horn, balm-horn, psalm-horn. . . .

They are hunting the goals that they understand:— *This section beginning*
sonorously, ending in a
San-Francisco and the brown sea-sand.   *languorous whisper.*

My goal is the mystery the beggars win.   135
I am caught in the web the night-winds spin.
The edge of the wheat-ridge speaks to me.
I talk with the leaves of the mulberry tree.
And now I hear, as I sit all alone
In the dusk, by another big Santa-Fé stone,   140
The souls of the tall corn gathering round
And the gay little souls of the grass in the ground.
Listen to the tale the cottonwood tells.
Listen to the windmills, singing o'er the wells.
Listen to the whistling flutes without price   145
Of myriad prophets out of paradise.
Harken to the wonder
That the night-air carries. . . .
Listen . . . to . . . the . . . whisper . . .
Of . . . the . . . prairie . . . fairies   150
    Singing o'er the fairy plain:—   *To the same whispered tune*
    "Sweet, sweet, sweet, sweet.   *as the Rachel-Jane song—*
    Love and glory,   *but very slowly.*
    Stars and rain,
    Sweet, sweet, sweet, sweet. . . ."   155

1. When this poem was written, the automobile was still a marvelous
   chariot. In your opinion, what was the poet's purpose in writing this
   poem? What did the Santa-Fé Trail represent to those pioneers who
   settled the West? What does it represent in this poem?

2. Point out the details in the poem which help you to picture what
   those early autos were like. From what Lindsay revealed about himself,
   what kind of person do you think he was? Cite evidence from the
   poem. What kind of life appealed to him? How do you interpret
   lines 47 and 48?

3. What goals do the drivers of the autos seek and understand? Why
   did the poet refer to his goal as "the mystery the beggars win"? What
   was "the wonder that the night-air carries"?

4. What is the setting of the poem—the place and the period in which
   the events occurred? From what point was the poet observing the
   world around him and watching the "United States" go by? From
   the descriptions of the horns (lines 79-87), what clues do you find to
   the kind of people traveling in the cars?

5. Note the various contrasts in the poem; for example, between the "smoke-black freights" and the autos; between the song of the Rachel-Jane and "all of the tunes" of the passing cars. What do the lines describing the Rachel-Jane song add to the total effect of the poem? What do you think this song symbolized for the poet?

6. Sounds are the very substance of this poem and of other Lindsay poems. To convey these sounds the poet has used almost every poetic device: rhythm, rhyme, and repetition; alliteration, assonance, and onomatopoeia. Point out examples of each which you found especially effective.

7. The poet identified this poem as "A Humoresque," a fanciful or humorous musical composition. Tell why you would, or would not, have chosen this term to describe this poem. Of course, you must first read the poem according to the poet's directions, in order to know how he intended it to sound.

The Leaden-Eyed

Let not young souls be smothered out before
They do quaint° deeds and fully flaunt their pride.   strange
It is the world's one crime its babes grow dull,
Its poor are ox-like, limp and leaden-eyed.

Not that they starve, but starve so dreamlessly,   5
Not that they sow, but that they seldom reap,
Not that they serve, but have no gods to serve,
Not that they die but that they die like sheep.

1. To whom was Lindsay referring in the title? What is "the world's one crime"? Show how stanza 2 makes specific the magnitude of this crime. In line 4, how do you interpret the word *poor*?

2. Even though this poem is more- traditional than many of Lindsay's poems, it reflects his interest in creating a dramatic effect through sound and rhythm. What method is used in stanza 2 to create a dramatic effect? Find examples of alliteration which intensify the effectiveness of the sound.

3. What images in stanza 1 enrich the main image in the title? In which phrases in stanza 2 is the main image further explored?

Edgar Lee Masters

Although a lawyer by vocation, Edgar Lee Masters was a prolific writer of both prose and poetry. He had already published a number of volumes of conventional verse before he brought out, in 1915, the *Spoon River Anthology*, a collection of first-person epitaphs. These were supposedly written by some two hundred men and women now "sleeping on the hill" in the imaginary town of Spoon River. Masters created both the town and its deceased inhabitants from his memories of two small river-towns in Illinois where he had lived as a boy.

At the time the *Anthology* first appeared, many readers felt that the picture of small-town life conveyed through the epitaphs was one-sided and rather shocking. Masters claimed that it was not. His experiences as a lawyer had convinced him that the picture usually presented was false and highly sentimental. His purpose was not to misrepresent. Rather, it was to reveal frankly and with realistic detail the hearts and minds of simple people looking back on the lives they had lived. Since 1915 the *Anthology* has appeared in many editions and several languages.

The Hill

Where are Elmer, Herman, Bert, Tom and Charley,
The weak of will, the strong of arm, the clown, the
    boozer, the fighter?
All, all, are sleeping on the hill.

One passed in a fever,
One was burned in a mine,   5

One was killed in a brawl,
One died in a jail,
One fell from a bridge toiling for children and wife—
All, all are sleeping, sleeping, sleeping on the hill.

Where are Ella, Kate, Mag, Lizzie and Edith,   10
The tender heart, the simple soul, the loud, the proud,
    the happy one?—
All, all, are sleeping on the hill.

One died in shameful child-birth,
One of a thwarted love,
One at the hands of a brute in a brothel,   15
One of a broken pride, in the search for heart's desire,
One after life in far-away London and Paris
Was brought to her little space by Ella and Kate and Mag—
All, all are sleeping, sleeping, sleeping on the hill.

Where are Uncle Isaac and Aunt Emily,   20
And old Towny Kincaid and Sevigne Houghton,
And Major Walker who had talked
With venerable men of the revolution?—
All, all, are sleeping on the hill.

They brought them dead sons from the war,   25
And daughters whom life had crushed,
And their children fatherless, crying—
All, all are sleeping, sleeping, sleeping on the hill.

Where is Old Fiddler Jones
Who played with life all his ninety years,   30
Braving the sleet with bared breast,
Drinking, rioting, thinking neither of wife nor kin,
Nor gold, nor love, nor heaven?
Lo! he babbles of the fish-frys of long ago,
Of the horse-races of long ago at Clary's Grove,   35
Of what Abe Lincoln said
One time at Springfield.

1. This poem serves as the introduction to *Spoon River Anthology*. Written in free verse, it has neither rhyme nor a regular rhythm. Instead, the rhythm is carefully adapted to the sense of the lines. Point out examples of rhythm changes and show how they are determined by, and contribute to, the meaning or sense.

2. Despite the absence of rhyme and regular rhythm, the poem has pattern and unity. What structural and poetic devices did Masters use in order to achieve this? Note, for example, the repetitions of lines, phrases, and sounds.

3. Is Old Fiddler Jones also "sleeping on the hill"? How do you interpret the last four lines?

Doc Hill

I went up and down the streets
Here and there by day and night,
Through all hours of the night caring for the poor
    who were sick.
Do you know why?
My wife hated me, my son went to the dogs.   5
And I turned to the people and poured out my love to them.
Sweet it was to see the crowds about the lawns on
    the day of my funeral,
And hear them murmur their love and sorrow.
But oh, dear God, my soul trembled, scarcely able
To hold to the railing of the new life   10
When I saw Em Stanton behind the oak tree
At the grave,
Hiding herself, and her grief!

1. Why did such crowds of people come to Doc Hill's funeral? What had made his life worth living?

2. In the last five lines, the mood of the poem changes completely. Why? Note the image in lines 9 and 10. What meaning and emotion does it convey?

Constance Hately

You praise my self-sacrifice, Spoon River,
In rearing Irene and Mary,
Orphans of my older sister!
And you censure Irene and Mary
For their contempt for me!   5
But praise not my self-sacrifice,
And censure not their contempt;
I reared them, I cared for them, true enough!—
But I poisoned my benefactions°   deeds of charity
With constant reminders of their dependence.   10

1. When Constance Hately was still alive, what had been the attitude
   of the Spoon River inhabitants toward her benefactions? What were
   these benefactions?
2. After death, what insight did she gain about herself and her benefactions? What lines and words convey this insight and her feelings
   about it? To whom does *their* refer in line 10?
3. Indirectly the poem conveys an important truth about the relationship
   between people who need help and those who give it. State in your
   own words what you think this truth is.

Judge Somers

How does it happen, tell me,
That I who was most erudite° of lawyers,   learned
Who knew Blackstone and Coke[1]
Almost by heart, who made the greatest speech
The court-house ever heard, and wrote   5
A brief that won the praise of Justice Breese—

---
[1] *Blackstone and Coke*, law books

How does it happen, tell me,
That I lie here unmarked, forgotten,
While Chase Henry, the town drunkard,
Has a marble block, topped by an urn,   10
Wherein Nature, in a mood ironical,
Has sown a flowering weed?

1. Why do you suppose the grave of Judge Somers was "unmarked"?
   Why is it ironical that the town drunkard had a fancy gravestone?
   What added irony is there in the "flowering weed"?
2. What reason can you give for the judge's feeling bitter? What would
   you think was the attitude of the poet toward the judge? In which
   words, phrases, and lines is this attitude expressed?

Trainor, The Druggist

Only the chemist can tell, and not always the chemist,
What will result from compounding
Fluids or solids.
And who can tell
How men and women will interact   5
On each other, or what children will result?
There were Benjamin Pantier and his wife,
Good in themselves, but evil toward each other:
He oxygen, she hydrogen,
Their son, a devastating fire.   10
I Trainor, the druggist, a mixer of chemicals,
Killed while making an experiment,
Lived unwedded.

1. What did Trainor reveal about himself by drawing an analogy between
   chemical compounds and human relationships? What reason is suggested for his never marrying? Why is it significant that he was killed
   while making an experiment?
2. What do you think was the nature of Trainor's relationship to the
   other townspeople? Would the poem be as effective if you were told
   more about Benjamin Pantier and his wife? Explain.

Knowlt Hoheimer

I was the first fruits of the battle of Missionary Ridge.
When I felt the bullet enter my heart
I wished I had staid at home and gone to jail
For stealing the hogs of Curl Trenary,
Instead of running away and joining the army.   5
Rather a thousand times the county jail
Than to lie under this marble figure with wings,
And this granite pedestal
Bearing the words, "*Pro Patria.*"
What do they mean, anyway?   10

1. To the people in Spoon River, Knowlt Hoheimer was a hero in one of
   the early crucial battles of the Civil War. What honor did they pay
   him? How did he feel about it?
2. Point out the wry humor in Knowlt Hoheimer's reason for going to
   war and in his final comment. What kind of person do you think
   he was?

Lydia Puckett

Knowlt Hoheimer ran away to the war
The day before Curl Trenary
Swore out a warrant through Justice Arnett
For stealing hogs.
But that's not the reason he turned a soldier.   5
He caught me running with Lucius Atherton.
We quarreled and I told him never again
To cross my path.
Then he stole the hogs and went to the war—
Back of every soldier is a woman.   10

1. Although Lydia Puckett considered herself an important person in Knowlt Hoheimer's life, he made no mention of her in his epitaph. How do you explain her giving a different reason for his going to war than he gave? Why would she want to be the cause of his going?

2. What did Lydia Puckett mean by her final comment?

Judge Selah Lively

Suppose you stood just five feet two,
And had worked your way as a grocery clerk,
Studying law by candle light
Until you became an attorney at law?
And then suppose through your diligence,   5
And regular church attendance,
You became attorney for Thomas Rhodes,
Collecting notes and mortgages,
And representing all the widows
In the Probate Court? And through it all   10
They jeered at your size, and laughed at your clothes
And your polished boots? And then suppose
You became the County Judge?
And Jefferson Howard and Kinsey Keene,
And Harmon Whitney, and all the giants   15
Who had sneered at you, were forced to stand
Before the bar and say "Your Honor"—
Well, don't you think it was natural
That I made it hard for them?

1. How did the judge justify his actions when "all the giants" were forced to stand before him at the bar? Why did he call them giants?

2. Note that the judge used the word *natural* to describe his treatment of the giants. What did he mean? Do you think the poet wanted you to sympathize with the judge? What words and phrases in the poem give you a clue to the poet's own feelings?

Davis Matlock

Suppose it is nothing but the hive:
That there are drones and workers
And queens, and nothing but storing honey—
(Material things as well as culture and wisdom)—
For the next generation, this generation never living,   5
Except as it swarms in the sun-light of youth,
Strengthening its wings on what has been gathered,
And tasting, on the way to the hive
From the clover field, the delicate spoil.
Suppose all this, and suppose the truth: 10
That the nature of man is greater
Than nature's need in the hive;
And you must bear the burden of life,
As well as the urge from your spirit's excess—
Well, I say to live it out like a god   15
Sure of immortal life, though you are in doubt,
Is the way to live it.
If that doesn't make God proud of you
Then God is nothing but gravitation,
Or sleep is the golden goal.   20

1. In lines 1-9, to what did Davis Matlock compare *it*; namely, the way this generation was living? What was the honey they all gathered? Why did he believe that this way of life was not the way to live (lines 11 and 12)?
2. What did Davis Matlock believe was the way to live life? What did he mean by the statement in the last three lines?

Father Malloy

You are over there, Father Malloy,
Where holy ground is, and the cross marks every grave,
Not here with us on the hill—
Us of wavering faith, and clouded vision
And drifting hope, and unforgiven sins.   5
You were so human, Father Malloy,
Taking a friendly glass sometimes with us,
Siding with us who would rescue Spoon River
From the coldness and the dreariness of village morality.
You were like a traveler who brings a little box of sand   10
From the wastes about the pyramids
And makes them real and Egypt real.
You were a part of and related to a great past,
And yet you were so close to many of us.
You believed in the joy of life.   15
You did not seem to be ashamed of the flesh.
You faced life as it is,
And as it changes.
Some of us almost came to you, Father Malloy,
Seeing how your church had divined the heart,   20
And provided for it,
Through Peter the Flame,
Peter the Rock.

1. Why wasn't Father Malloy "sleeping" with the others? Why do you
    think the poet had the "others" give Father Malloy's epitaph for him?
    In what ways did they feel he was different from them? What do their
    comments reveal about their own past lives?
2. What idea is expressed in the simile in lines 10-12? How did the poet
    give lines 10-12 and 22-23 special importance by his choice and arrange-
    ment of words?
3. Reread lines 20 and 21. What do they mean, particularly the phrase
    "divined the heart"? Tell what you think this poem reveals about
    Masters' attitude toward "village morality."

Carl Sandburg

The poetry of Carl Sandburg echoes the sound and rhythm of Whitman's poetry, and carries forward Whitman's pioneering poetic style. It also reflects Whitman's understanding of, and concern for, the common man. However, Sandburg has never been a slavish imitator. He knew first hand the folk wisdom and the feelings of those Americans of mixed heritage with whom he grew up in the brawling, expanding, optimistic Middle West. It was from these people that he gathered both the subject matter and the language of his poetry. Before he became a reporter in Chicago, he had worked at all sorts of manual tasks, meeting people from many walks of life and coming to appreciate their courage and determination. When he has called them "Comrades," he has not used the word in either a sentimental or ideological sense. He has meant only to express his feeling of oneness with them.

When *Chicago Poems*, Sandburg's first volume of verse, was published in 1916, it attracted considerable attention. Yet his style was so different from that of the traditional poets that many readers were reluctant to accept his verse as poetry. Not until the publication of the next volumes of verse—*Cornhuskers* (1918), *Smoke and Steel* (1920), and *Slabs of the Sunburnt West* (1922)—was his reputation as poetic spokesman for the common man firmly established.

Sandburg's last two volumes of verse, *Good Morning, America* and *The People, Yes*, have a quieter, more pensive quality than the earlier volumes. They are full of the distilled wisdom of the common man as it expresses itself in homely proverbs and folk songs. The years which Sandburg devoted to the six-volume life of Abraham Lincoln gave him a turn of mind very like that of his hero: a strange mixture of common sense with compassion and melancholy.

The People Will Live On

The people will live on.
The learning and blundering people will live on.
    They will be tricked and sold and again sold
And go back to the nourishing earth for rootholds,
    The people so peculiar in° renewal and **comeback**,   uniquely capable of   5
    You can't laugh off their capacity to take it.
The mammoth rests between·his cyclonic dramas.

The people so often sleepy, weary, enigmatic,°   puzzling
is a vast huddle with many units saying:
    "I earn my living   10
    I make enough to get by
    and it takes all my time.
    If I had more time
    I could do more for myself
    and maybe for others.   15
    I could read and study
    and talk things over
    and find out about things.
    It takes time.
    I wish I had the time."   20

The people is a tragic and comic two-face:
hero and hoodlum: phantom and gorilla twist-
ing to moan with a gargoyle mouth: "They
buy me and sell me ... it's a game ...
sometime I'll break loose ..."   25

    Once having marched
Over the margins of animal necessity,
Over the grim line of sheer subsistence
    Then man came
To the deeper rituals of his bones,   30
To the lights lighter than any bones,

To the time for thinking things over,
To the dance, the song, the story,
Or the hours given over to dreaming,
    Once having so marched.   35

Between the finite limitations of the five senses
and the endless yearnings of man for the beyond
the people hold to the humdrum bidding of work and food
while reaching out when it comes their way
for lights beyond the prison of the five senses,   40
for keepsakes lasting beyond any hunger or death.
    This reaching is alive.
The panderers and liars have violated and smutted it.
    Yet this reaching is alive yet
    for lights and keepsakes.   45

    The people know the salt of the sea
    and the strength of the winds
    lashing the corners of the earth.
    The people take the earth
    as a tomb of rest and a cradle of hope.   50
    Who else speaks for the Family of Man?
    They are in tune and step
    with constellations of universal law.

    The people is a polychrome,°   many-colored thing
    a spectrum and a prism   55
    held in a moving monolith,°   uniform mass
    a console organ of changing themes,
    a clavilux° of color poems   color-making instrument
    wherein the sea offers fog
    and the fog moves off in rain   60
    and the Labrador sunset shortens
    to a nocturne of clear stars
    serene over the shot spray
    of northern lights.

    The steel mill sky is alive.   65
    The fire breaks white and zigzag
    shot on a gun-metal gloaming.

Man is a long time coming.
Man will yet win.
Brother may yet line up with brother: 70

This old anvil laughs at many broken hammers.
        There are men who can't be bought.
        The fireborn are at home in fire.
        The stars make no noise.
        You can't hinder the wind from blowing.   75
        Time is a great teacher.
        Who can live without hope?

In the darkness with a great bundle of grief
        the people march.
In the night, and overhead a shovel of stars for   80
        keeps, the people march:
                        "Where to? What next?"

1. On what did Sandburg base his belief that "the people will live on"?
    What are they reaching for "beyond the prison of the five senses"?
    What "lights and keepsakes" are worth the "humdrum bidding of
    work and food"?

2. In what predicament did the "vast huddle" of people find itself? What
    did it wish for? Why was it "a tragic and comic two-face"?

3. What had man's yearning for the "beyond" led him to discover? What
    did the poet mean by the statement in lines 42-45? Who and what
    keep man from maintaining this state? Why do you think man wants it?

4. What is the anvil in line 71? Do you think the proverbs in stanza 9
    represent the "many broken hammers"? Explain.

5. What uncommon image of the sky is developed in stanzas 8 and 10?
    In stanza 3, what picture of man is conveyed by the images? How
    would you characterize the diction of the poem?

6. In your opinion, what is the over-all idea or theme of this poem? Do
    you think that the "vast huddle" of people today march "in the dark-
    ness with a great bundle of grief"?

7. What reason can you see for the shape of the poem; namely, the
    indentation of certain lines. Can you see any relationship beween the
    purpose served by the long lines and that served by the indented lines?
    Discuss.

Psalm of Those Who Go Forth Before Daylight

The policeman buys shoes slow and careful; the teamster buys gloves slow and careful; they take care of their feet and hands; they live on their feet and hands.

The milkman never argues; he works alone and no one speaks to him; the city is asleep when he is on the job; he puts a bottle on six hundred porches and calls it a day's work; he climbs two hundred wooden stairways; two horses are company for him; he never argues.

The rolling-mill men and the sheet-steel men are brothers of cinders; they empty cinders out of their shoes after the day's work; they ask their wives to fix burnt holes in the knees of their trousers; their necks and ears are covered with a smut; they scour their necks and ears; they are brothers of cinders.

1. The Biblical psalms are hymns in praise or honor of God. Why do you think that Sandburg chose these people to honor or praise? What attitudes and qualities of character do they represent? Are these men different from those who go forth in the daytime? Find evidence for your answers in the poem.
2. Each stanza of this poem resembles a short, one-sentence paragraph. Yet Sandburg was writing poetry. Point out the poet's choice of language, the repetitions, and the rhythm which are more characteristic of poetry than of prose.

personification - strong burly man.

Chicago

Hog Butcher for the World,
Tool Maker, Stacker of Wheat,
Player with Railroads and the Nation's Freight Handler;
    Stormy, husky, brawling,
    City of the Big Shoulders: 5

They tell me you are wicked and I believe them, for I have seen
    your painted women under the gas lamps luring the farm
    boys.
And they tell me you are crooked and I answer: Yes, it is true I
    have seen the gunman kill and go free to kill again.

Al Capone

And they tell me you are brutal and my reply is: On the faces
    of women and children I have seen the marks of wanton
    hunger.
And having answered so I turn once more to those who sneer at
    this my city, and I give them back the sneer and say to
    them:
Come and show me another city with lifted head singing so
    proud to be alive and coarse and strong and cunning.   10
Flinging magnetic curses amid the toil of piling job on job, here
    is a tall bold slugger set vivid against the little soft cities;
Fierce as a dog with tongue lapping for action, cunning as a
    savage pitted against the wilderness,
      Bareheaded,
      Shoveling,
      Wrecking,   15
      Planning,
      Building, breaking, rebuilding.
Under the smoke, dust all over his mouth, laughing with white
    teeth,
Under the terrible burden of destiny laughing as a young man
    laughs,

Laughing even as an ignorant fighter laughs who has never lost a
    battle,   20
Bragging and laughing that under his wrist is the pulse, and
    under his ribs the heart of the people,
Laughing!
Laughing the stormy, husky, brawling laughter of Youth, half-
    naked, sweating, proud to be Hog Butcher, Tool Maker,
    Stacker of Wheat, Player with Railroads and Freight Han-
    dler to the Nation.

1. Was Sandburg criticizing or defending this city that he knew so well? Who are *they* in line 6? Why did they sneer? What did he challenge them to do?

2. As what is the city personified? What metaphors did Sandburg use to portray the character, appearance, and actions of the person with whom the city is compared? Which metaphors do you consider most effective?

3. Note the emphasis given the single word *Laughing* by placing it on a separate line. What reason can you give for the poet's emphasizing this word? Considering the city's "terrible burden of destiny," why would it laugh? What clues in the poem suggest that destiny?

4. Compare the first and last stanzas. How are they similar and different? What effect is achieved by beginning and ending the poem in much the same way?

5. There is a strong rhythm in the poem, but it is not determined by the usual combinations of accented and unaccented syllables. Rather it is determined by the meaning of the lines and the rhythm of speech. Demonstrate this rhythm by reading the poem aloud.

Threes

I was a boy when I heard three red words
a thousand Frenchmen died in the street
for: Liberty, Equality, Fraternity—I asked
why men die for words.

I was older; men with mustaches, sideburns,   5
lilacs, told me the high golden words are:
Mother, Home, and Heaven—other older men with
face decorations said: God, Duty, Immortality
—they sang these threes slow from deep lungs.

Years ticked off their say-so on the great clocks   10
of doom and damnation, soup and nuts: meteors flashed
their say-so: and out of great Russia came three
dusky syllables workmen took guns and went out to die
for: Bread, Peace, Land.

And I met a marine of the U.S.A., a leatherneck with   15
a girl on his knee for a memory in ports circling the
earth and he said: Tell me how to say three things
and I always get by—gimme a plate of ham and eggs—
how much?—and—do you love me, kid?

1. At various times in history, men and nations have found different words
   to express what they valued. Why were the three words in stanza 1
   described as "red"? On what occasion did men die for them? Why
   would dying for words seem strange to a young boy?
2. What clues are you given in stanza 2 that help you picture the time
   and place of "the high golden words"? What do the two groups of
   words reveal about the values of the time and the way of life? What
   did they mean to those who spoke or sang them?
3. Note the change of mood in stanza 3. What has been happening in
   the world as the "years ticked off their say-so"? Why are the three

single-syllable words described as "dusky"? Why did they matter so much to Russia that "workmen took guns and went out to die" for them?

4. What values are conveyed by the "three things" in stanza 4? What commentary on life was Sandburg making in this poem? Was he suggesting that to die for words—or what the words stand for—has always been foolish and romantic? Was he suggesting that the values of modern man—represented by those of the marine—are superficial and selfish? You may consider neither of these interpretations satisfactory. Base your opinion both on the ideas presented in the poem and on the words and phrases that convey the poet's attitude.

Happiness

I asked professors who teach the meaning of life to tell me what
    is happiness.
And I went to famous executives who boss the work of thousands
    of men.
They all shook their heads and gave me a smile as though I was
    trying to fool with them.
And then one Sunday afternoon I wandered out along the
    Desplaines river
And I saw a crowd of Hungarians under the trees with their
    women and children and a keg of beer and an accordion.   5

1. Do you think the poet was implying that he discovered the meaning of happiness on his walk? What would have led him to believe the Hungarians were happy?
2. How had the professors and executives responded when he consulted them? What is ironic about the fact that they didn't seem to know?
3. Suppose that the poet had asked the Hungarians, "What is happiness?" How do you think they would have responded? Can happiness ever be defined in words? Is the purpose of the poem to suggest that it cannot be defined? Is it to suggest that the people who ought to know what happiness means either do not know it or do not consider it important to know it? State what you think is the purpose, basing your opinion on a thoughtful interpretation of the poem.

Cool Tombs

When Abraham Lincoln was shoveled into the tombs, he forgot
the copperheads[1] and the assassin . . . in the dust, in the cool
tombs.

And Ulysses Grant lost all thought of con men and Wall Street,
cash and collateral turned ashes . . . in the dust, in the cool
tombs.

Pocahontas' body, lovely as a poplar, sweet as a red haw[2] in
November or a pawpaw in May, did she wonder? does she
remember? . . . in the dust, in the cool tombs?

Take any streetful of people buying clothes and groceries, cheering a hero or throwing confetti and blowing tin horns . . . tell
me if the lovers are losers . . . tell me if any get more than the
lovers . . . in the dust . . . in the cool tombs.

---

[1] *copperheads,* Northerners sympathizing with the South during the Civil War
[2] *haw,* hawthorn berry

1. Each of the three people named in the poem was famous in a different
   way. What comfort did the "cool tombs" bring to Lincoln and Grant?
   Why, and in what way, did the "cool tombs" affect Pocahontas? What
   might she have wondered about and what might she have remembered?
2. What kind of people was Sandburg talking about in the last stanza?
   When the time came for them also to be "shoveled into the tombs,"
   which of them would *not* be "losers"? Do you think that the poet was
   implying that the three famous people were, or were not, also lovers?
3. What is the effect of the repetition at the end of the lines? How is
   this varied in line 4? What is the effect of this variation?

Robinson Jeffers

Robinson Jeffers was a regional poet of California in the same sense that Robert Frost was a regional poet of New England. The setting and imagery in Jeffers' poems reflect his love for the rocky California coastal country, but the themes of his poems are universal. In all he wrote there is a deep and frequently furious pessimism, which he expressed in a free verse reminiscent of Walt Whitman.

Jeffers' poems are generally more tortured than those of his contemporaries. He viewed modern man as a horror of violence, fraud, and hatred. To escape from man, he fled to nature, the source of beauty and strength; yet, even in nature he found violence and brutality. In his poetry, nature is never portrayed as placid and pastoral. It, too, shares the evil he found in civilization. Nevertheless, he believed that the one hope for man was an anti-rational absorption in the natural world. In human action he saw little purpose or progress.

Hurt Hawks

I

The broken pillar of the wing jags from the clotted shoulder,
The wing trails like a banner in defeat,
No more to use the sky forever but live with famine
And pain a few days: cat nor coyote
Will shorten the week of waiting for death, there is game
    without talons.   5
He stands under the oak-bush and waits
The lame feet of salvation; at night he remembers freedom
And flies in a dream, the dawns ruin it.

He is strong and pain is worse to the strong, incapacity
   is worse.
The curs of the day come and torment him   10
At distance, no one but death the redeemer will humble
   that head,
The intrepid readiness, the terrible eyes.
The wild God of the world is sometimes merciful to those
That ask mercy, not often to the arrogant.
You do not know him, you communal people, or you have
   forgotten him;   15
Intemperate and savage, the hawk remembers him;
Beautiful and wild, the hawks, and men that are dying,
   remember him.

II

I'd sooner, except the penalties, kill a man than a hawk; but
   the great redtail
Had nothing left but unable misery
From the bone too shattered for mending, the wing that
   trailed under his talons when he moved.   20
We had fed him six weeks, I gave him freedom,
He wandered over the foreland hill and returned in the
   evening, asking for death,
Not like a beggar, still eyed with the old
Implacable arrogance. I gave him the lead gift in the twilight.
   What fell was relaxed,   25
Owl-downy, soft feminine feathers; but what
Soared: the fierce rush: the night-herons by the flooded river
   cried fear at its rising
Before it was quite unsheathed from reality.

1. From his experiences with two hawks—one who waited for death and
    one to whom he brought death—Jeffers revealed the beauty and strength
    he found in nature as well as the violence and brutality. What suffer-
    ings did the first hawk (Part I) have to endure while waiting for death?
    Why would no cat or coyote shorten the waiting? Why was "the wild
    God of the world" not merciful to him? Why are pain and incapacity
    worse for the strong than for the weak?

2. The hawks, and men who are dying, remember "the wild God of the world," yet he is unknown or forgotten by the "communal people." Why? What attitude toward nature and people is conveyed in Part I?

3. What reason can you find in the poem for the poet's statement in the first line of Part II? In spite of the poet's strong feelings, he finally gave the redtail hawk "the lead gift." Why? What made the night-herons cry "fear"? What view of life and death is conveyed in lines 25-28?

4. To get the full effect and meaning of Jeffers' images requires careful reading of such phrases as "lame feet of salvation" (line 7) and "unable misery" (line 19). What thought and feeling does each convey? Find other images and discuss their effect.

Boats in a Fog

Sports and gallantries, the stage, the arts, the antics of
    dancers,
The exuberant voices of music,
Have charm for children but lack nobility; it is bitter
    earnestness
That makes beauty; the mind
Knows, grown adult.   5
               A sudden fog-drift muffled the ocean,
A throbbing of engines moved in it,
At length, a stone's throw out, between the rocks and the
    vapor,
One by one moved shadows
Out of the mystery, shadows, fishing-boats, trailing each
    other   10
Following the cliff for guidance,
Holding a difficult path between the peril of the sea-fog
And the foam on the shore granite.
One by one, trailing their leader, six crept by me,
Out of the vapor and into it,   15
The throb of their engines subdued by the fog, patient and
    cautious,

Coasting all round the peninsula
Back to the buoys in Monterey harbor. A flight of pelicans
Is nothing lovelier to look at;
The flight of the planets is nothing nobler; all the arts lose
    virtue   20
Against the essential reality
Of creatures going about their business among the equally
Earnest elements of nature.

1. Is the title the real subject of the poem? What was the poet attempt-
   ing to make clear? Why wouldn't the mind, "grown adult," accept as
   beauty "what have charm for children"?
2. What impressed the poet about the passage of the boats? To what did
   he compare them? What conclusions did he draw and why?
3. Explain the meaning of the poet's final statement, beginning "all the
   arts lose virtue" (line 20). Is this the same meaning he expressed in
   lines 3 and 4?
4. Do you think that the first five lines of the poem would, or would not,
   have been equally effective at the end of the poem? Give reasons for
   your answer.

To the Stone-Cutters

Stone-cutters fighting time with marble, you fore-defeated
Challengers of oblivion
Eat cynical earnings, knowing rock splits, records fall down,
The square-limbed Roman letters
Scale in the thaws, wear in the rain. The poet as well   5
Builds his monument mockingly;
For man will be blotted out, the blithe earth die, the brave sun
Die blind and blacken to the heart:
Yet stones have stood for a thousand years, and pained
    thoughts found
The honey of peace in old poems.   10

1. In what way are the stone-cutters and the poet alike? Why are the first "fore-defeated challengers"? Why does the poet "build his monument mockingly"? What fate awaits man?

2. Is there any justification for the stone-cutters and the poet to continue their work? In what lines is this expressed?

3. Note the words *cynical* (line 3) and *mockingly* (line 6). What attitude on the part of the poet do they suggest? Is this attitude consistent throughout, even in the concluding lines? Explain.

Rock and Hawk

Here is a symbol in which
Many high tragic thoughts
Watch their own eyes.

This gray rock, standing tall
On the headland, where the seawind   5
Lets no tree grow,

Earthquake-proved, and signatured
By ages of storms: on its peak
A falcon has perched.

I think, here is your emblem   10
To hang in the future sky;
Not the cross, not the hive,

But this; bright power, dark peace;
Fierce consciousness joined with final
Disinterestedness;   15

Life with calm death; the falcon's
Realist eyes and act
Married to the massive

> Mysticism of stone,
> Which failure cannot cast down   20
> Nor success make proud.

1. What two objects combine to make up the symbol referred to in line 1? What qualities does each of the two represent? Point out the words and phrases which identify these qualities.
2. In your opinion, what reason did Jeffers have for believing that the combination of rock and hawk is a better emblem to hang "in the future sky" than the cross or the hive?
3. What did Jeffers mean in the last two lines of the poem?

The World's Wonders

Being now three or four years more than sixty,
I have seen strange things in my time. I have seen a merman
    standing waist-deep in the ocean off my rock shore,

Unmistakably human and unmistakably a sea-beast: he sub-
    merged and never came up again,
While we stood watching. I do not know what he was, and I have
    no theory: but this was the least of wonders.

I have seen the United States grow up the strongest and wealth-
    iest of nations, and swim in the wind over bankruptcy.   5
I have seen Europe, for twenty-five hundred years the crown of
    the world, become its beggar and cripple.

I have seen my people, fooled by ambitious men and a froth of
    sentiment, waste themselves on three wars.
None was required, all futile, all grandly victorious. A fourth is
    forming.

I have seen the invention of human flight; a chief desire of man's
    dreaming heart for ten thousand years;
And men have made it the chief of the means of massacre.   10

I have seen the far stars weighed and their distance measured,
    and the powers that make the atom put into service—
For what?—To kill. To kill half a million flies—men I should say
    —at one slap.

I have also seen doom. You can stand up and struggle or lie down
    and sleep—you are doomed as Oedipus.[1]
A man and a civilization grow old, grow fatally—as we say—ill:
    courage and the will are bystanders.

It is easy to know the beauty of inhuman things, sea, storm and
    mountain; it is their soul and their meaning.   15
Humanity has its lesser beauty, impure and painful; we have to
    harden our hearts to bear it.

I have hardened my heart only a little: I have learned that happi-
    ness is important, but pain gives importance.
The use of tragedy: Lear[2] becomes as tall as the storm he crawls
    in; and a tortured Jew became God.

---

[1] *Oedipus,* in the Sophocles tragedy, is moved by fate to pluck out his eyes
[2] *Lear,* in the Shakespeare tragedy, goes mad in a storm

1. On what did Jeffers base his conclusion that to bear the beauty of
   humanity "we have to harden our hearts"? How does this beauty differ
   from that of inhuman things?
2. From his consideration of "the world's wonders," what did Jeffers
   learn? Note especially his use of the words *important* and *importance*
   (line 17). How is this truth supported by the examples given in the
   last line of the poem?
3. Why was the merman described in stanzas 1 and 2 as "the least of the
   wonders"? How did Jeffers feel about the wonders described in stanzas
   3-6? Which words and comments reveal his feelings? What reason do
   you have for thinking that the tone of these four stanzas is, or is not,
   ironical?
4. Re-read stanza 7. Did Jeffers see any hope for man and for civilization?
   How do you think he meant these lines to be interpreted?
5. Much of the effect of this poem is due to the repetition of phrases
   and of opening words of consecutive stanzas. Point out examples of
   these and of similar devices which convey the poet's grim and pessi-
   mistic mood as he recalls the "world's wonders" he has seen.

Amy Lowell

In the years just preceding 1914, a group of poets in London were attracted and stimulated by an American expatriate named Ezra Pound. This group came to be known as the "Imagist" school, and included among its followers a number of other expatriate Americans. Amy Lowell, a member of one of New England's most famous "upper-crust" families, was one of these.

At first Miss Lowell's relationship with Pound was one of pleasant enmity, for two such domineering personalities "could not get on in the same boat." When they quarreled over the editorship of the Imagists' anthology, Pound withdrew from the Imagist group and Miss Lowell became its spokesman in both England and America. Combining poetic skill with a crusading organizational drive, she made "Imagism" practically a household word in this country.

The Imagists' guidelines for the writing of poetry, which seemed, at that time, an attack on all poetry then in print, naturally stirred up quite a furor in the United States, but out of the ensuing discussion came a clearer understanding of the nature of the new poetry. Today these same guidelines seem neither shocking nor revolutionary. Rather, they impress one merely as sensible rules for any poet to follow:

To present an image that is sharp and precise
To use the language of common speech
To employ the exact word, not the merely decorative word
To create new rhythms to express new moods, usually using free verse
To allow absolute freedom in the choice of subject matter
To produce poetry that is hard and clear, not blurred and indefinite
To strive for concentration, avoiding all unnecessary words and phrases.

The poets who followed these guidelines brought new vigor to the poetry of the time—a new look for a new spirit. Amy Lowell herself, although a proclaimed Imagist, experimented with many different poetic forms, from the highly concentrated, stylized word images of the Orient to the Shakespearean sonnet.

Night Clouds

The white mares of the moon rush along the sky
Beating their golden hoofs upon the glass Heavens;
The white mares of the moon are all standing on their hind legs
Pawing at the green porcelain doors of the remote Heavens.
Fly, mares!   5
Strain your utmost,
Scatter the milky dust of stars,
Or the tiger sun will leap upon you and destroy you
With one lick of his vermilion tongue.

1. The images in this poem grow out of the comparisons implied in two metaphors. What are these metaphors? Tell why you do, or do not, consider them effective.

2. Which images picture the movement of the clouds? Which picture the consequences if the clouds do not heed the warning? What words and phrases convey color and action? Are they important to the total effect? Explain.

3. Refer to the guidelines of the Imagists on page 112. Find evidence in the poem for as many of these guidelines as you can.

Patterns

I walk down the garden paths,
And all the daffodils
Are blowing,° and the bright blue squills.°   blooming; early spring flowers
I walk down the patterned garden-paths
In my stiff, brocaded gown.   5
With my powdered hair and jewelled fan,
I too am a rare
Pattern. As I wander down
The garden paths.

My dress is richly figured,   10
And the train
Makes a pink and silver stain
On the gravel, and the thrift
Of the borders.
Just a plate of current fashion,   15
Tripping by in high-heeled, ribboned shoes.
Not a softness anywhere about me,
Only whalebone and brocade.
And I sink on a seat in the shade
Of a lime tree. For my passion   20
Wars against the stiff brocade.
The daffodils and squills
Flutter in the breeze
As they please.
And I weep;   25
For the lime-tree is in blossom
And one small flower has dropped upon my bosom.

And the plashing of waterdrops
In the marble fountain
Comes down the garden-paths.   30
The dripping never stops.

Underneath my stiffened gown
Is the softness of a woman bathing in a marble basin,
A basin in the midst of hedges grown
So thick, she cannot see her lover hiding,   35
But she guesses he is near,
And the sliding of the water
Seems the stroking of a dear
Hand upon her.
What is Summer in a fine brocaded gown!   40
I should like to see it lying in a heap upon the ground.
All the pink and silver crumpled up on the ground.

I would be the pink and silver as I ran along the paths,
And he would stumble after,
Bewildered by my laughter.   45
I should see the sun flashing from his sword-hilt and the
    buckles on his shoes.
I would choose
To lead him in a maze along the patterned paths,
A bright and laughing maze for my heavy-booted lover.
Till he caught me in the shade,   50
And the buttons of his waistcoat bruised my body as he
    clasped me,
Aching, melting, unafraid.
With the shadows of the leaves and the sundrops,
And the plopping of the waterdrops,
All about us in the open afternoon—   55
I am very like to swoon
With the weight of this brocade,
For the sun sifts through the shade.

Underneath the fallen blossom
In my bosom,   60
Is a letter I have hid.
It was brought to me this morning by a rider from the
    Duke.
"Madam, we regret to inform you that Lord Hartwell
Died in action Thursday se'nnight."°   a week ago
As I read it in the white, morning sunlight,   65

The letters squirmed like snakes.
"Any answer, Madam," said my footman.
"No," I told him.
"See that the messenger takes some refreshment.
No, no answer."   70
And I walked into the garden,
Up and down the patterned paths,
In my stiff, correct brocade.
The blue and yellow flowers stood up proudly in the sun,
Each one.   75
I stood upright too,
Held rigid to the pattern
By the stiffness of my gown.
Up and down I walked,
Up and down.   80

In a month he would have been my husband.
In a month, here, underneath this lime,
We would have broke the pattern;
He for me, and I for him,
He as Colonel, I as Lady,   85
On this shady seat.
He had a whim
That sunlight carried blessing.
And I answered, "It shall be as you have said."
Now he is dead.   90

In Summer and in Winter I shall walk
Up and down
The patterned garden-paths
In my stiff, brocaded gown.
The squills and daffodils   95
Will give place to pillared roses, and to asters, and to snow.
I shall go
Up and down,
In my gown.
Gorgeously arrayed,   100
Boned and stayed.

And the softness of my body will be guarded from embrace
By each button, hook, and lace.
For the man who should loose me is dead,
Fighting with the Duke in Flanders,   105
In a pattern called a war.
Christ! What are patterns for?

1. The theme of "Patterns"—the clash between individual desire and
    convention—had been used by earlier poets. Miss Lowell presented it
    in a dramatic monologue, the speaker an eighteenth-century lady. What
    did this lady tell you about herself that justified her statement, "I too
    am a rare pattern"? Why did her passion war against the stiff brocade?
    What reason did she have for weeping?

2. As the lady walked in the garden, she imagined a meeting which might
    have taken place if she had given expression to her feelings. What pro-
    test is expressed in lines 40 and 41? What does "a fine brocaded gown"
    symbolize?

3. In lines 59-61, the lady revealed the reason for her walking up and
    down the patterned paths. What clues to her feelings can you find in
    her reaction to the letter, in her remarks to the footman, and in her
    comment about the blue and yellow flowers?

4. What did the lady mean in lines 84-89? Discuss the full implication
    of line 90.

5. Is the mood of the last stanza resigned, desperate, angry, defeated? Is
    it similar to, or different from, the mood of the entire poem?

6. Much of the meaning of the poem depends on the interpretation of
    the word *pattern*. In lines 7 and 8, the lady referred to herself as a
    "pattern"; in line 106, to war as a "pattern." Find other uses of the
    word in the poem, as a noun or as an adjective. Give the interpretation
    you think the poet intended to convey. Do not overlook her grief-
    stricken question in the final line of the poem.

7. This poem exemplifies most, if not all, of the guidelines set forth by
    the Imagists. (See page 112.) Point out several examples in the poem
    which you consider particularly effective illustrations of each guideline.
    Also point out those poetic devices which are used by traditional poets
    as well as the "new poets"; for example, repetition of words and
    phrases, alliteration, rhyme, short lines for emphasis.

Red Slippers

Red slippers in a shop-window; and outside in the street, flaws of gray, windy sleet!

Behind the polished glass the slippers hang in long threads of red, festooning from the ceiling like stalactites[1] of blood, flooding the eyes of passers-by with dripping color, jamming their crimson   5
reflections against the windows of cabs and tram-cars, screaming their claret and salmon into the teeth of the sleet, plopping their little round maroon lights upon the tops of umbrellas.

The row of white, sparkling shop-fronts is gashed and bleeding, it bleeds red slippers. They spout under the electric light, fluid   10
and fluctuating, a hot rain—and freeze again to red slippers, myriadly multiplied in the mirror side of the window.
They balance upon arched insteps like springing bridges of crimson lacquer; they swing up over curved heels like whirling tanagers sucked in a wind-pocket; they flatten out, heelless, like   15
July ponds, flared and burnished by red rockets.
Snap, snap, they are cracker sparks of scarlet in the white, monotonous block of shops.
They plunge the clangor of billions of vermilion trumpets into the crowd outside, and echo in faint rose over the pavement.   20

People hurry by, for these are only shoes, and in a window farther down is a big lotus bud of cardboard, whose petals open every few minutes and reveal a wax doll, with staring bead eyes and flaxen hair, lolling awkwardly in its flower chair.
One has often seen shoes, but whoever saw a cardboard lotus   25
bud before?

The flaws of gray, windy sleet beat on the shop-window where there are only red slippers.

---

[1] *stalactites*, rock formations dripping from ceilings of limestone caves

1. Why do the people hurry past the shop-window containing the red slippers? What did the poet find so fascinating about this shop-window that she tried to capture in words?

2. What effect did the flaws of gray, windy sleet have on what the poet saw or imagined as she looked into the window or at the world outside the window? Note that the slippers "hang in long threads of red." They are unmoving, yet the poet's description of her impressions is full of movement—even of sound. Point out the images which convey both movement and sound.

3. The last line is almost an echo of the first, but the change in word order and in one or two words conveys a different meaning and especially a different mood. Show how both were developed in the course of the poem.

4. In appearance, the paragraph form of the poem is reminiscent of some of Whitman's poems. Suppose Miss Lowell had arranged her images in stanza form. Would the effect have seemed more poetic? Explain.

Ombre Chinoise[1]

Red foxgloves against a yellow wall streaked with plum-
    colored shadows;
A lady with a blue and red sunshade;
The slow dash of waves upon a parapet.
That is all.
Non-existent—immortal—   5
As solid as the center of a ring of fine gold.

-----
[1] *Ombre Chinoise*, Chinese shadows—possibly Chinese shadow puppets

In your opinion, do the images in lines 1-3 picture what the poet imagined or what she saw? Why do you think she referred to them as "non-existent" and "immortal"? To what was she referring in the last line? Was she suggesting that what the eye sees is no more real than what the eye cannot see? Was she suggesting that since the world is merely a person's impressions of it, these impressions live on? Work out the meaning you find most satisfying.

Lilacs

Lilacs,
False blue,
White,
Purple,
Color of lilac,   5
Your great puffs of flowers
Are everywhere in this my New England.
Among your heart-shaped leaves
Orange orioles hop like music-box birds and sing
Their little weak soft songs;   10
In the crooks of your branches
The bright eyes of song sparrows sitting on spotted eggs
Peer restlessly through the light and shadow
Of all Springs.
Lilacs in dooryards   15
Holding quiet conversations with an early moon;
Lilacs watching a deserted house
Settling sideways into the grass of an old road;
Lilacs, wind-beaten, staggering under a lopsided shock of
      bloom
Above a cellar dug into a hill.   20
You are everywhere.
You were everywhere.
You tapped the window when the preacher preached his
      sermon,
And ran along the road beside the boy going to school.
You stood by pasture-bars to give the cows good milking,   25
You persuaded the housewife that her dishpan was of silver
And her husband an image of pure gold.
You flaunted the fragrance of your blossoms
Through the wide doors of Custom Houses—
You, and sandal-wood, and tea,   30
Charging the noses of quill-driving clerks
When a ship was in from China.

You called to them: "Goose-quill men, goose-quill men,
May is a month for flitting,"
Until they writhed on their high stools   35
And wrote poetry on their letter-sheets behind the
      propped-up ledgers.
Paradoxical New England clerks,
Writing inventories in ledgers, reading the "Song of Solomon"
      at night,
So many verses before bed-time,
Because it was the Bible.   40
The dead fed you
Amid the slant stones of graveyards.
Pale ghosts who planted you
Came in the night-time
And let their thin hair blow through your clustered stems.   45
You are of the green sea,
And of the stone hills which reach a long distance.
You are of elm-shaded streets with little shops where they
      sell kites and marbles,
You are of great parks where everyone walks and nobody is
      at home.
You cover the blind sides of greenhouses   50
And lean over the top to say a hurry-word through the glass
To your friends, the grapes, inside.

Lilacs,
False blue,
White,   55
Purple,
Color of lilac,
You have forgotten your Eastern origin,
The veiled women with eyes like panthers,
The swollen, aggressive turbans of jewelled Pashas.   60
Now you are a very decent flower,
A reticent flower,
A curiously clear-cut, candid flower,
Standing beside clean doorways,
Friendly to a house-cat and a pair of spectacles,   65
Making poetry out of a bit of moonlight
And a hundred or two sharp blossoms.

Maine knows you,
Has for years and years;
New Hampshire knows you,   70
And Massachusetts
And Vermont.
Cape Cod starts you along the beaches to Rhode Island;
Connecticut takes you from a river to the sea.
You are brighter than apples,   75
Sweeter than tulips,
You are the great flood of our souls
Bursting above the leaf-shapes of our hearts,
You are the smell of all Summers,
The love of wives and children,   80
The recollection of the gardens of little children,
You are State Houses and Charters
And the familiar treading of the foot to and fro on a road
        it knows.
May is lilac here in New England,
May is a thrush singing "Sun up!" on a tip-top ash-tree,   85
May is white clouds behind pine-trees
Puffed out and marching upon a blue sky.
May is a green as no other,
May is much sun through small leaves,
May is soft earth,   90
And apple-blossoms,
And windows open to a South wind.
May is a full light wind of lilac
From Canada to Narragansett Bay.

Lilacs,   95
False blue,
White,
Purple,
Color of lilac.
Heart-leaves of lilac all over New England,   100
Roots of lilac under all the soil of New England,
Lilac in me because I am New England,
Because my roots are in it,
Because my leaves are of it,
Because my flowers are for it,   105

Because it is my country
And I speak to it of itself
And sing of it with my own voice
Since certainly it is mine.

1. A number of Miss Lowell's poems seem to have as their purpose the creation, through images, of a series of related impressions. What would you say was the purpose of "Lilacs"? Why did the poet identify herself with the lilac? What reasons did she give in the last stanza?

2. Note the poet's use of the apostrophe (see page 205) in stanzas 1 and 2, and the use of you when describing the lilac. What device did she use in lines 16 and 17? Find other examples and explain the effect they have on the tone of the poem and the sense of action they contribute to the poem.

3. What picture of lilacs in New England led the poet to comment "You are everywhere" (line 21)? To what period in New England life was she referring in lines 22-45? How did the lilacs affect the villagers, and particularly the New England clerks? What clue to the great age of the lilacs is given in lines 41-45?

4. In stanza 2, what contrast is drawn between the New England lilac and its Eastern ancestor?

5. How did the poet suggest the gradual spread of the lilac over the years and all the things with which it has become associated? What reason can you give for the shift in line 84 to a description of the month of May?

6. Note that stanzas 2 and 4 are of equal length and similar in pattern. At what point might the poet have divided stanza 1 (ending with line 32) to make a new stanza to match 2 and 4?

7. The rhythmical flow of this poem—and of many free-verse poems—depends more on cadence than on meter. Cadence is the effect created by the rise and fall of the voice and by the emphasis and pause required by the meaning. In other words, the rhythm is not determined by a carefully planned combination of accented and unaccented syllables, as in traditional verse. Rather it is determined by the pattern of accents natural to speech and to the meaning intended by the poet. Choose a portion of the poem you enjoyed and read it aloud. Note the rhythmical effect achieved through cadence rather than through traditional meter.

8. The images in this poem have charm as well as sharpness and precision; for example, the lilacs leaning over the top of the greenhouse "to say a hurry-word" to the grapes. There are many others. Point out your favorites.

H. D.

H. D. was the signature of Hilda Doolittle, one of the earliest members of the Imagist group and, judging by her work, the one who remained most faithful to its ideals. The outstanding characteristic of her verse, as of all true Imagist verse, is an intense concentration of expression. Her method in writing a poem was to focus on a single experience and, through the evocative power of clear, concrete images, to recreate that experience, interpret it, and convey its emotional impact on her.

Like all Imagist poetry, the poems of H. D. are impressionistic and subjective. Through a single word-picture she captured an experience or moment and gave it permanence. Through her response to it—frequently intense—she gave it life.

Song

You are as gold
as the half-ripe grain
that merges to gold again,
as white as the white rain
that beats through   5
the half-opened flowers
of the great flower tufts
thick on the black limbs
of an Illyrian[1] apple bough.

Can honey distil such fragrance   10
as your bright hair—

---

[1] *Illyrian.* Ancient Illyria corresponded geographically to present-day Albania.

for your face is as fair as rain,
yet as rain that lies clear
on white honey-comb
lends radiance to the white wax,   15
so your hair on your brow
casts light for a shadow.

1. To whom was the poet speaking? What picture of this person did the images create in your mind?
2. Note that most of the images are created by means of similes. In stanza 1, what comparisons convey the qualities of the gold and the white? In stanza 2, what comparisons convey fragrance and fairness? How do you interpret the external image in lines 13-17?
3. Although this poem is written in free verse, the poet has made use of rhyming. Point out examples of end rhyme, near rhyme, and eye rhyme.

Oread

Whirl up, sea—
whirl your pointed pines,
splash your great pines
on our rocks,
hurl your green over us—   5
cover us with your pools of fir.

1. The title—a Greek word meaning "mountain nymph"—identifies the speaker in the poem. The mood and the images are created by a simple metaphor. What are they? In your opinion, is the implied comparison effective or over-done? Explain.
2. What do you think is the purpose of the poem? How is this achieved through concentration and the use of the exact word? Would a fuller description have conveyed a clearer impression? Explain.

The Garden

I

You are clear,
O rose, cut in rock;
hard as the descent of hail.

I could scrape the color
from the petals,   5
like spilt dye from a rock.

If I could break you
I could break a tree.

If I could stir
I could break a tree—   10
I could break you.

II

O wind, rend open the heat,
cut apart the heat,
rend it to tatters.

Fruit cannot drop   15
through this thick air;
fruit cannot fall into heat
that presses up and blunts
the points of pears,
and rounds the grapes.   20

Cut the heat:
plough through it,
turning it on either side
of your path.

1. What experience was the poet describing in this poem? What clues in Part I tell you the mood of the poet? Why did the rose seem to be "cut in rock"? How do you think that stanzas 3 and 4 should be interpreted?

2. In Part II the poet appealed to the wind. Why did she want it to cut apart the heat? What relationship do you see between the ideas and mood in Part II and those in Part I?

3. Are the images intended to picture a scene or experience or to convey the poet's mood and feelings? Explain.

4. What qualities does this poem have which the Imagists considered important? (See page 112.)

Orchard

I saw the first pear
as it fell—
the honey-seeking, golden-banded,
the yellow swarm,
was not more fleet than I,   5
(Spare us from loveliness!)
and I fell prostrate,
crying:
you have flayed us with your blossoms;
spare us the beauty   10
of fruit-trees!

The honey-seeking
paused not;
the air thundered their song,
and I alone was prostrate.   15

O rough-hewn
god of the orchard,
I bring you an offering;
do you, alone unbeautiful

son of the god,   20
spare us from loveliness.

These fallen hazel-nuts,
stripped late of their green sheaths;
grapes, red-purple,
their berries   25
dripping with wine;
pomegranates already broken,
and shrunken figs,
and quinces untouched,
I bring you as offering.   30

1. Why did the speaker in the poem bring an offering to Pan, the god of the orchard? Why did she fall prostrate and cry out when she saw the first pear fall? What "yellow swarm" was not more fleet than she? To whom was her cry addressed?

2. In lines 6 and 21, the poet made the same plea. What is this "loveliness"? Why did she say, "Spare us" from it? To whom does us refer?

3. How was her offering to Pan different from the beauty from which she wanted to be spared?

William Carlos Williams

By birth and habitation, Williams was a city person. As a doctor in Rutherford, New Jersey, he developed a love for the diversity of people who live in this industrialized area near New York City. This love and a sensitive ear for the varied rhythms of human speech supplied him with the subject matter and the language of his poetry.

During his days as a medical student at the University of Pennsylvania, Williams came under the influence of Ezra Pound, a fellow student and budding poet, who later brought Williams temporarily into the fold of the Imagists. (See page 112.) His desire to elaborate his ideas, and to develop a structure suitable to their expression, soon carried him out of the confines of the Imagist school, although he never completely escaped its influence. Nearly all of his poems are written in free verse and in the language of the common man. With each successive volume, his poetry has become less traditional in structure and idea and more experimental and radical. In some poems he seems to be using language to achieve an effect similar to that achieved by the non-representational painters of the 1920's and 1930's.

The Forgotten City

When I was coming down from the country
with my mother, the day of the storm,
trees were across the road and small branches
kept rattling on the roof of the car.
There was ten feet or more of water   5
making the parkways impassable with the wind

bringing more rain in sheets. Brown torrents
gushed up through new sluiceways in the
valley floor so that I had to take any road
I could find bearing to the south and west,   10
to get back to the city. I passed through
extraordinary places, as vivid as any
I ever saw where the storm had broken
the barrier and let through
a strange commonplace: Long, deserted avenues   15
with unrecognized names at the corners and
drunken looking people with completely
foreign manners. Monuments, institutions
and in one place a large body of water
startled me with an acre or more of hot   20
jets spouting up symmetrically over it. Parks.
I had no idea where I was and promised
myself I would some day go back to study
this curious and industrious people who lived
in these apartments, at these sharp   25
corners and turns of intersecting avenues
with so little apparent communication
with an outside world. How did they get
cut off this way from representation in our
newspapers and other means of publicity   30
when so near the metropolis, so closely
surrounded by the familiar and the famous?

1. What setting and situation are described in the first 15 lines? To
   what does "the barrier" (line 14) refer? What did the poet mean
   by "a strange commonplace" (line 15)?

2. In lines 22 and 23 the poet promised himself he would someday go
   back to this unknown place. Why? What puzzled him most? What
   clue are you given in the title? In what sense is the city a forgotten
   city?

3. Tell why you do, or do not, think the language of this poem resembles
   the language of everyday speech. What lines or phrases—if any—
   impress you as different? Comment on the choice and arrangement
   of the words, and on the sentence structure and punctuation.

Pastoral

When I was younger
it was plain to me
I must make something of myself.
Older now
I walk back streets   *double meaning*   5
admiring the houses
of the very poor: *(because they are of vast import)*
roof out of line with sides
the yards cluttered
with old chicken wire, ashes,   10
furniture gone wrong;
the fences and outhouses
built of barrel-staves
and parts of boxes, all,
if I am fortunate,   15
smeared a bluish green — *color of the old fences.*
that properly weathered
pleases me best — *because he is admiring the city*
of all colors.

　　　No one   20
will believe this — *slum*
of vast import to the nation.

without slums people wouldn't be happy with what they have. Come from slums — gave urge to push forward be better off than they are.

1. As the poet used the word *pastoral* he might have been referring (1) to shepherds, their work or way of life, or (2) to a rural scene or way of life. As you choose between these meanings, keep in mind that the poet was also a doctor. How does this explain lines 1-3 and the reason why, "older now," he admires the houses of the very poor?

2. What meaning do you think is intended in line 15? To what does *this* refer in line 21? What was the poet saying in lines 20-22? Was he serious or somewhat amused? Explain.

The Crowd at the Ball Game

The crowd at the ball game
is moved uniformly

by a spirit of usefulness
which delights them—

all the exciting detail   5
of the chase

and the escape, the error
the flash of genius—

all to no end save beauty
the eternal—   10

So in detail they, the crowd,
are beautiful

for this
to be warned against

saluted and defied—   15
It is alive, venomous

it smiles grimly
its words cut—

The flashy female with her
mother, gets it—   20

The Jew gets it straight—it
is deadly, terrifying—

It is the Inquisition, the
Revolution

It is beauty itself   25
that lives

day by day in them
idly—

This is
the power of their faces   30

It is summer, it is the solstice
the crowd is

cheering, the crowd is laughing
in detail

permanently, seriously   35
without thought

1. In this poem Williams is concerned not with the appearance of the crowd but rather with its reactions and the reasons for these reactions. In what ways is a crowd "useful" to the game being played? What must be "warned against, saluted and defied"?

2. What mood and emotions are conveyed in lines 16-18? How are they related to what the Jew felt—remembering past persecution—and to the Inquisition and the Revolution?

3. The term beauty is usually associated with what is pleasing. Yet in many works of art the painter or writer has captured the beauty of violence, death, destruction, even human destitution and ugliness. What do you think Williams meant by the word beauty as he used it in this poem?

4. What interpretation of lines 25-26 do you think is in keeping with the ideas and mood brought out earlier in the poem?

5. The structure of the poem adds interest but makes the reading difficult. Point out those lines in which meaning requires the reader to continue into the next line or stanza without a break.

Burning the Christmas Greens

Their time past, pulled down
cracked and flung to the fire
—go up in a roar

All recognition lost, burnt clean
clean in the flame, the green   5
dispersed, a living red,
flame red, red as blood wakes
on the ash—

and ebbs to a steady burning
the rekindled bed become   10
a landscape of flame

At the winter's midnight
we went to the trees, the coarse
holly, the balsam and
the hemlock for their green   15

At the thick of the dark
the moment of the cold's
deepest plunge we brought branches
cut from the green trees

to fill our need, and over   20
doorways, about paper Christmas
bells covered with tinfoil
and fastened by red ribbons

we stuck the green prongs
in the windows hung   25
woven wreaths and above pictures
the living green. On the

mantel we built a green forest
and among those hemlock
sprays put a herd of small   30
white deer as if they

were walking there. All this!
and it seemed gentle and good
to us. Their time past,
relief! The room bare. We   35

stuffed the dead grate
with them upon the half burntout
log's smoldering eye, opening
red and closing under them

and we stood there looking down.   40
Green is a solace
a promise of peace, a fort
against the cold (though we

did not say so) a challenge
above the snow's   45
hard shell. Green (we might
have said) that, where

small birds hide and dodge
and lift their plaintive
rallying cries, blocks for them   50
and knocks down

the unseeing bullets of
the storm. Green spruce boughs
pulled down by a weight of
snow—Transformed!   55

Violence leaped and appeared.
Recreant!° roared to life   yielding up, surrendering
as the flame rose through and
our eyes recoiled from it.

In the jagged flames green   60
to red, instant and alive. Green!
those sure abutments° ... Gone!   supports
lost to mind

and quick° in the contracting   alive
tunnel of the grate   65
appeared a world! Black
mountains, black and red—as

yet uncolored—and ash white,
an infant landscape of shimmering
ash and flame and we, in   70
that instant, lost,

breathless to be witnesses,
as if we stood
ourselves refreshed among
the shining fauna of that fire.   75

1. In the first three stanzas, what scene is pictured? Whose time is past? What is meant by "the green dispersed"? What "wakes on the ash"?

2. What event did the poet recollect in lines 12-32? What need was filled by this gathering of the greens? How does the image "winter's midnight" help to picture the season and the weather? Point out similar images in the following stanza and the impressions they create.

3. When the greens were in place, how did the decorators feel? What idea and feeling is conveyed in the line "their time past, relief!"?

4. What did "'green" represent to those who watched the burning branches? What pictures did it bring to mind? What "new world" appeared "in the contracting tunnel of the grate"? How do you interpret the last stanza?

5. Note that Williams used a device generally associated with the short story; namely, a flashback. What event did he recreate that occurred at an earlier time? How did this help you to understand and appreciate the meaning which the burning of the greens had for those who took part in it?

6. This poem clearly illustrates the influence of the Imagists on Williams

and also his desire to develop a structure suitable to the expression of
his ideas. What reason can you see for his use of capitals in lines 4, 12,
and 16 but no period until line 27? What effect is created by these
"on-flowing" lines and the short sentences in stanzas 9, 14, 15, and 16?
Point out the images which impressed you most and the pictures they
create in the mind.

In Chains

When blackguards and murderers
under cover of their offices
accuse the world of those villainies
which they themselves invent to
torture it—we have no choice   5
but to bend to their designs,
buck them or be trampled while
our thoughts gnaw, snap and bite
within us helplessly—unless
we learn from that to avoid   10
being as they are, how love
will rise out of its ashes if
we water it, tie up the slender
stem and keep the image of its
lively flower chiseled upon our minds.   15

1. Whom do you think the poet was referring to as "blackguards and
   murderers"? How do you interpret line 2? Who are the "we" in line
   5? Why are all the choices named in the poem useless?
2. What did the poet suggest was our only hope? To what does that
   refer in line 10? What relation do you see between not "being as they
   are" and the "love" pictured in lines 11-15? Are the ashes from which
   love will rise its own? Are they the ashes of the past before we learned?
   What clues do you think suggest the answer?
3. What did the poet mean by "the image of its lively flower"? Why
   must we keep it "chiseled upon our minds"?
4. What reason can you see for the poet's choosing "In Chains" as the
   title for this poem?

The Words Lying Idle

The fields parched, the leaves
drying on the maples, the birds' beaks
gaping! if it would rain,
if it would only rain! Clouds come up,
move from the west and from the south   5
but they bring no rain. Heat and dry winds
—the grass is curled and brittle underfoot,
the foot leaves it broken. The roads are dust.

But the mind is dust also
and the eyes burn from it. They burn more   10
from restless nights, from the full moon shining
on a dry earth than from lack of rain.
The rain, if it fell, would ease the mind
more than the grass, the mind would
be somewhat, at least, appeased against   15
this dryness and the death implied.

1. What details in stanza 1 dramatize the effect of the continued drought on nature and on the speaker in the poem? What mood is conveyed by the words "if it would only rain!"?

2. What did the poet mean by the opening statement in stanza 2? What suffering would be eased "if it would only rain"?

3. At first the title seems to have little relation to the idea of the poem or to the mood. Yet it is in these "words" that the speaker in the poem expressed his feelings as he observed the suffering caused by the drought. Why did he speak of these words as "lying idle"? What is the meaning of idle in "idle talk" and in "idle hands"? Are the two meanings similar or different? Tell which meaning you think the poet intended to convey in his use of idle in the title. Or did he intend to convey both or neither? Explain.

EXPERIMENTERS WITH
LANGUAGE

IN the twenties and early thirties, there was a resurgence of experimentation among American poets. The prescriptions of the Imagists, which had seemed revolutionary and liberating in the preceding decade, now seemed outworn and restrictive. The "realistic" verse of such socially minded poets as Carl Sandburg—the poetic counterpart of early twentieth-century realistic prose—also seemed to have served its purpose. The time had come for poets to seek a different direction for American verse. The time had come, in Ezra Pound's words, to "make it new."

The early leaders in this search—and the spiritual fathers of most young poets today—were Ezra Pound and T. S. Eliot,[1] both Midwesterners with Eastern education and European tastes. Because they considered American culture stifling and American poetry second-rate, Pound and Eliot sought inspiration and guidance in the older, allegedly more coherent European literary tradition. Both

---

[1] The editor regrets that permission to include any of T. S. Eliot's poems in this paperback volume could not be secured.

chose the modes of earlier ages and of foreign cultures to express their special, private responses to the modern world.

To identify Pound, Eliot, and their contemporaries as experimenters with language does not mean that they have not also experimented with rhythm, figures of speech, and even with rhyme. Their common preoccupation, however, has been to explore the possibilities of language as language, a concern shared by most American poets of the last three decades. Each in his own way has sought combinations of words capable of *suggesting*—through overtone and ambiguity —the complexity of his private perceptions and special reactions to contemporary life.

Ezra Pound

As early as 1916, when Harriet Monroe's magazine *Poetry* was still new, Ezra Pound was an important influence in the development of the "new poetry." His first volumes of verse—published soon after his arrival in London in 1909—made a definite impression on the critics, and it was largely through his efforts that the Imagists emerged as a group in 1913. When Amy Lowell replaced him as spokesman for the group, he served as foreign correspondent for *Poetry* and as London editor of *The Little Review*. He then moved to Paris and later to Italy, "constantly escaping somewhere," as one critic has said, "in an effort to find himself." He was also constantly searching for new subject matter, often in classical, medieval, and oriental literature. His treatment of it was often so unconventional that his poetry never won wide public acceptance. In fact, he has been called " a poet for poets," and it was for his distinguished service to American letters that he received the *Dial* Award in 1927.

Unlike the traditionalist poets, and even the experimenters with form, Pound was primarily interested in using language not to clarify and heighten meaning but rather to evoke impressions, emotions, and associations. He assigned to the reader the responsibility for relating these and for deriving from them the meaning of the poem. In a number of Pound's poems—and particularly in the *Cantos*—the reader cannot *fully* grasp the meaning unless he is familiar with the literary and artistic sources to which Pound alludes or from which he has drawn his subject matter.

The Garden

En robe de parade.[1] Samain

Like a skein of loose silk blown against a wall
She walks by the railing of a path in Kensington Gardens,[2]
And she is dying piece-meal
    of a sort of emotional anemia.

And round about there is a rabble   5
Of the filthy, sturdy, unkillable infants of the very poor.
They shall inherit the earth.

In her is the end of breeding.
Her boredom is exquisite and excessive.
She would like someone to speak to her,   10
And is almost afraid that I
    will commit that indiscretion.

———

[1] En robe de parade, finely dressed
[2] Kensington Gardens, gardens in the heart of London

1. What kind of woman is portrayed in the poem? What clue to her
   appearance and manner is provided in the simile (lines 1 and 2)?
   What response to life is conveyed in lines 3-4 and 9?

2. What reason can you see for the description of the "rabble" in stanza
   2? Note the contrast between the idea expressed in line 9 and that
   in line 8.

3. What additional insight into the woman's personality and attitude
   do you gain from the last two lines? Do you think she is afraid,
   haughty, suspicious? Where in the poem does the poet reveal how he
   felt toward her as he observed her in "the garden"?

The Tree

I stood still and was a tree amid the wood,
Knowing the truth of things unseen before;
Of Daphne and the laurel bow
And that god-feasting couple old
That grew elm-oak amid the wold.°   wood   5
'Twas not until the gods had been
Kindly entreated, and been brought within
Unto the hearth of their heart's home
That they might do this wonder thing;
Nathless° I have been a tree amid the wood   nevertheless   10
And many a new thing understood
That was rank folly to my head before.

1. The people referred to in this poem are characters in Greek mythology. Daphne, a nymph, was changed into a laurel tree to escape the pursuing god, Apollo. The god-feasting couple were Baucis and Philemon. As a reward for their hospitality to the disguised gods Zeus and Hermes, they were immortalized as twin trees. By what means did the poet discover "the truth of things unseen"? In your opinion what was this "truth"? To what do you think he was referring in lines 11 and 12?

2. In lines 6-9, was the poet suggesting that the gods might "do this wonder thing" only under special conditions? What were they? Do you think these conditions represent one of the new things he came to understand? Was the experience presented here a real mystical experience, or imaginary? Explain.

3. This poem has some of the characteristics of free verse and of rhymed verse. If there is a predominant rhythm, what is it? Which lines illustrate it? In which lines does the cadence rather than the meter determine the rhythm?

4. Can you see any reason for the rhyming of certain lines, but not of others? Tell why you do, or do not, consider this poem free verse. What effect is created by the poet's use of repetition of phrases and of vowel sounds? Find examples.

The Return

See, they return; ah, see the tentative
    Movements, and the slow feet,
    The trouble in the pace and the uncertain
    Wavering!

See, they return, one, and by one,   5
With fear, as half-awakened;
As if the snow should hesitate
And murmur in the wind,
        and half turn back;
These were the "Wing'd-with-Awe,"   10
    Inviolable.°   **beyond harm**

Gods of the wingèd shoe!
With them the silver hounds,
    sniffing the trace of air!

Haie! Haie!°   **hunting cry** 15
    These were the swift to harry;
These the keen-scented;
These were the souls of blood.

Slow on the leash,
    pallid the leash-men!   20

1. What impression of the "returning" is conveyed in lines 1-9? Note
particularly such words as *half-awakened* (line 6) and the simile in
lines 7-9. Discuss the images they create in the mind.
2. Are "these" in lines 10-18 the same people as the "returning"? How
do you account for the very different impressions created in these
lines? What makes you think that the poet was recalling what he had
seen at an earlier time? What clues in the poem suggest the time and
circumstances?

3. Point out the phrases that create the dramatic contrast between the
   picture of the "returning" and that of the "Wing'd-with-Awe."
4. Where do you think that the "returning" had been with their silver
   hounds? To whom was Pound referring in lines 19 and 20? Why did
   he refer to them as "leash-men"? Do you think the poem is merely
   a picture of the return of a hunting party, or do you think the hunters
   represent a group of men returning from some enterprise such as war
   or from some battle against the forces of nature? Discuss.

Night Litany

O Dieu, purifiez nos cœurs![1]
         Purifiez nos cœurs!

Yea the lines hast thou laid unto me
         in pleasant places,
And the beauty of this thy Venice   5
         hast thou shown unto me
Until is its loveliness become unto me
         a thing of tears.

O God, what great kindness
         have we done in times past   10
         and forgotten it,
That thou givest this wonder unto us,
         O God of waters?

O God of the night,
         What great sorrow   15
Cometh unto us,
         That thou thus repayest us
Before the time of its coming?

O God of silence,
         Purifiez nos cœurs,   20
         Purifiez nos cœurs,

---

[1] O Dieu, . . . coeurs! Oh God, purify our hearts!

For we have seen
The glory of the shadow of the
            likeness of thine handmaid,

Yea, the glory of the shadow   25
            of thy Beauty hath walked
Upon the shadow of the waters
In this thy Venice.
            And before the holiness
Of the shadow of thy handmaid   30
      Have I hidden mine eyes,
            O God of waters.

O God of silence,
            Purifiez nos cœurs,
            Purifiez nos cœurs,   35
O God of waters,
            make clean our hearts within us,
            For I have seen the
Shadow of this thy Venice
Floating upon the waters,   40
            And thy stars

Have seen this thing; out of their far courses
Have they seen this thing,
            O God of waters,
Even as are thy stars   45
Silent unto us in their far-coursing,
Even so is mine heart
            become silent within me.

            Purifiez nos cœurs
O God of the silence,   50
            Purifiez nos cœurs
O God of waters.

1. A litany is a prayer of supplication in which the clergy and the con-
gregation may take turns in reciting the parts. Here the poet speaks

both parts. What is the "wonder" which God had given him? Why did he speak of its loveliness as "a thing of tears"? In lines 9-18, what did he suggest as possible reasons for the gift?

2. What relationship do you see between the poet's hiding his eyes and the "glory of the shadow" described in lines 23-32?

3. Why did the poet feel so intensely the need for purification of the heart? Why did he address his supplication to the "God of silence" and the "God of waters"? How are they associated with the "wonder" referred to in lines 12 and 13? Is each God mentioned in the poem a different God or merely one aspect of the single God whose gift he is praising? Explain.

4. What experience had the poet and the stars shared? What likeness did he see between their response and that of his heart? What emotions do you think the poet felt as he recited this "Night Litany"?

5. The language of the poem is not the language of everyday speech. What likeness do you see between it and the language of the Church? Note, for example, the use of yea (lines 3 and 25), the archaic cometh and givest, the rhythm of lines 23-26, and the repetition of words and phrases. Find other examples and describe their effect on the tone of the poem and your response to it. In your opinion, is the tone a part of the meaning? How does the repeated supplication "Purifiez nos coeurs" contribute to that tone and meaning?

Further Instructions

Come, my songs, let us express our baser passions.
Let us express our envy for the man with a steady job
    and no worry about the future.

You are very idle, my songs;
I fear you will come to a bad end.   5

You stand about the streets.
You loiter at the corners and bus-stops.
You do next to nothing at all.

You do not even express our inner nobilities;
You will come to a very bad end.   10

And I? I have gone half cracked.
I have talked to you so much
    that I almost see you about me,
Insolent little beasts! Shameless! Devoid of clothing!

But you, newest song of the lot,   15
You are not old enough to have done much mischief.
I will get you a green coat out of China
With dragons worked upon it.
I will get you the scarlet silk trousers
From the statue of the infant Christ at Santa Maria Novella;   20
Lest they say we are lacking in taste,
Or that there is no caste° in this family.   status

1. What reason do you have for thinking that this speaker is a dis-
   couraged poet? Why is he dissatisfied with the "songs" he has
   already written? What makes him think he has "gone half cracked"?

2. In stanza 5, the speaker in the poem says of his newest song (1) that
   it is not old enough to have done much mischief, and (2) that he
   will dress it in elegant clothes. How do you interpret these comments?
   Who is "they" in line 21? Who are "we" and "this family" in lines
   21 and 22?

3. In your opinion, is this a light or serious poem? Do you think the
   speaker in the poem is poking fun at himself, his poetry, and the
   poetry-reading public? Discuss.

from Canto 1

Pound was as famous for his poetic translations of ancient works as for his original poems. Here he has used as his source a Latin translation of an episode from Homer's *Odyssey*. In this episode, Odysseus journeys to the land of the dead to learn his fate from the prophet Tiresias. The ship and supplies are provided by Circe, the famous enchantress, and it is by following her directions that Odysseus succeeds in his mission.

And then went down to the ship,
Set keel to breakers, forth on the godly sea, and
We set up mast and sail on that swart° ship,   dark
Bore sheep aboard her, and our bodies also
Heavy with weeping, and winds from sternward   5
Bore us out onward with bellying canvas,
Circe's this craft, the trim-coifed goddess.
Then sat we amidships, wind jamming the tiller,
Thus with stretched sail, we went over sea till day's end.
Sun to his slumber, shadows o'er all the ocean,   10
Came we then to the bounds of deepest water,
To the Kimmerian[1] lands, and peopled cities
Covered with close-webbed mist, unpierced ever
With glitter of sun-rays
Nor with stars stretched, nor looking back from heaven   15
Swartest night stretched over wretched men there.
The ocean flowing backward, came we then to the place
Aforesaid by Circe.
Here did they rites, Perimedes and Eurylochus,
And drawing sword from my hip   20
I dug the ell-square pitkin;°   small pit
Poured we libations° unto each the dead,   sacrificial drinks
First mead and then sweet wine, water mixed with white flour.

---

[1] *Kimmerian.* In Homeric legend, the Cimmerians lived in a remote region of mist and gloom.

Then prayed I many a prayer to the sickly death's-heads;
As set in Ithaca, sterile bulls of the best   25
For sacrifice, heaping the pyre with goods,
A sheep to Tiresias[2] only, black and a bell-sheep.
Dark blood flowed in the fosse,°   trench
Souls out of Erebus,[3] cadaverous dead, of brides
Of youths and of the old who had borne much;   30
Souls stained with recent tears, girls tender,
Men many, mauled with bronze lance heads,
Battle spoil, bearing yet dreary arms,
These many crowded about me; with shouting,
Pallor upon me, cried to my men for more beasts;   35
Slaughtered the herds, sheep slain of bronze;
Poured ointment, cried to the gods,
To Pluto the strong, and praised Proserpine;[4]
Unsheathed the narrow sword,
I sat to keep off the impetuous impotent dead,   40
Till I should hear Tiresias.
But first Elpenor came, our friend Elpenor,
Unburied, cast on the wide earth,
Limbs that we left in the house of Circe,
Unwept, unwrapped in sepulcher, since toils urged other.   45
Pitiful spirit. And I cried in hurried speech:
"Elpenor, how art thou come to this dark coast?
"Cam'st thou afoot, outstripping seamen?"
            And he in heavy speech:
"Ill fate and abundant wine. I slept in Circe's ingle.°   fireside nook 50
"Going down the long ladder unguarded,
"I fell against the buttress,
"Shattered the nape-nerve, the soul sought Avernus.[5]
"But thou, O King, I bid remember me, unwept, unburied,
"Heap up mine arms, be tomb by sea-bord,° and inscribed: sea-shore 55
"A man of no fortune, and with a name to come.
"And set my oar up, that I swung mid fellows."

---

[2] Tiresias, a blind soothsayer from Thebes
[3] Erebus, gloomy space through which souls passed to Hades
[4] Pluto . . . Proserpine, the god and goddess of the Underworld
[5] Avernus, Hades

And Anticlea came, whom I beat off, and then Tiresias
  Theban,
Holding his golden wand, knew me, and spoke first: 60
"A second time? why? man of ill star,
"Facing the sunless dead and this joyless region?
"Stand from the fosse, leave me my bloddy bever°   drink
"For soothsay."°   prophecy
           And I stepped back,   65
And he strong with the blood, said then: "Odysseus
"Shalt return through spiteful Neptune, over dark seas,
"Lose all companions." And then Anticlea came. . . .

1. From the details in the poem, what directions do you think that
   Circe gave Odysseus? What did Tiresias require before he would
   prophesy? How was this provided? Why did Odysseus have to stand
   guard over it?

2. Why did Odysseus call Elpenor "pitiful spirit"? What request did
   Elpenor make? Why did the fulfillment of this request mean so much
   to him?

3. In this translation, as in the original version, the descriptions of the
   time and place, the ceremonies, and the actions and feelings of
   Odysseus are as essential to the story as the events. Discuss the
   impressions you gained of each of these from the poem.

4. Originally the adventures of Odysseus were recounted by a bard to
   the accompaniment of a lyre. As you read the first nine lines aloud,
   note the grouping of the lines and the resulting cadence. What is
   unusual about the arrangement of the words? Point out examples of
   words and arrangements of words which impressed you as interesting
   and effective.

Archibald MacLeish

Archibald MacLeish's total contribution to the development of modern American poetry is difficult to assess because it has taken so many forms. Besides producing a sizable body of first-rate verse himself, he has served as a kind of ambassador-at-large for more experimental poets. He has helped to make the reading public aware of new experiments in form and language by championing them publicly and by exploiting them in his own poems, which tend otherwise to be more traditional than those of his contemporaries. Because he has acted on his belief that artists must accept a degree of social responsibility, he has shown that modern poetry need not be private, precious, and obscure.

In keeping with his conviction that the purpose of art is to communicate, he has tended to use a language based more on the spoken word than on conventional poetic diction. His verse forms range from traditional stanzaic patterns to free verse. His imagery—in which he excels—is always vivid, and often moving.

Ever Since

What do you remember thinking back?
What do you think of at dusk in the slack
Evening when the mind refills
With the cool past as a well fills in
Darkness from forgotten rains?   5

Do you think of waking in the all-night train,
The curtains drawn, the Mediterranean
Blue, blue, and the sellers of oranges
Holding heaped up morning toward you?

Do you think of Kumomoto-Ken   10
And the clogs° going by in the night and the scent of   wooden
                                                            shoes
Clean mats, the sound of the peepers,°   frogs
The wind in the pines, the dark sleep?

Do you think how Santiago stands at
Night under its stars, under its Andes: 15
Its bells like heavy birds that climb
Widening circles out of time?

I saw them too. I know those places.
There are no mountains—scarcely a face
Of all the faces you have seen,   20
Or a town or a room, but I have seen it.

Even at dusk in the deep chair
Letting the long past take you, bear you—
Even then you never leave me, never can.
Your eyes close, your small hands   25
Keep their secrets in your lap:
Wherever you are we two were happy.

I wonder what those changing lovers do,
Watching each other in the darkening room,
Whose world together is the night they've shared: 30
Whose past is parting: strangers side by side.

1. To whom is this poem addressed? At what point in the poem were you certain of the identity of the "you"? What reason did the speaker in the poem have for saying, "you never leave me, never can"?

2. What led the speaker to wonder about "those changing lovers" (line 28)? How did he feel about them? Why was his feeling toward the "you" so much different? Compare the reference to the past in line 31 with that in line 4. What impression do you gain of the happy lovers from the details given in the poem?

3. In stanzas 1-4 the speaker pictured the sights, sounds, and smells which the "you" might have remembered, thinking back. The unusual words, figures of speech, and images which convey these impressions also convey the mood of the poem and the feelings of the speaker. Note, for example, the simile in lines 3 and 4, and the image in lines 8 and 9. Why are these effective? Find others.

4. Even in the first line, the reader is aware of the strong rhythm of the poem. Is it a cadence based on meaning or a regular pattern based on poetic feet? Explain.

5. In addition to occasional end rhymes (point these out), the poet has rhymed just the accented syllable in the end word, as in lines 3 and 4. Find other examples. Do you think these add to, or detract from, the melodious effect of the poem? Explain.

Brave New World

But you, Thomas Jefferson
You could not lie so still,
You could not bear the weight of stone
On the quiet hill,

You could not keep your green grown peace 5
Nor hold your folded hand

If you could see your new world now,
Your new sweet land.

There was a time, Tom Jefferson,
When freedom made free men.   10
The new found earth and the new freed mind
Were brothers then.

There was a time when tyrants feared
The new world of the free.
Now freedom is afraid and shrieks   15
At tyranny.

Words have not changed their sense so soon
Nor tyranny grown new.
The truths you held, Tom Jefferson,
Will still hold true.   20

What's changed is freedom in this age.
What great men dared to choose
Small men now dare neither win
Nor lose.

Freedom, when men fear freedom's use   25
But love its useful name,
Has cause and cause enough for fear
And cause for shame.

We fought a war in freedom's name
And won it in our own.   30
We fought to free a world and raised
A wall of stone.

Your countrymen who could have built
The hill fires of the free
To set the dry world all ablaze   35
With liberty—

To burn the brutal thorn in Spain
Of bigotry and hate

And the dead lie and the brittle weed
Beyond the Plate:[1]   40

Who could have heaped the bloody straw,
The dung of time, to light
The Danube in a sudden flame
Of hope by night—

Your countrymen who could have hurled   45
Their freedom like a brand
Have cupped it to a candle spark
In a frightened hand.

Freedom that was a thing to use
They've made a thing to save   50
And staked it in and fenced it round
Like a dead man's grave.

You, Thomas Jefferson,
You could not lie so still,
You could not bear the weight of stone   55
On your green hill,

You could not hold your angry tongue
If you could see how bold
The old stale bitter world plays new
And the new world old.   60

---

[1] *Plate*, river in South America

1. Why do you think this poem was addressed to Jefferson? If he could
   see his "new world now," why would it disturb his "green grown
   peace"? What did the poet mean by the statements in lines 21-24?
2. What evidence did the poet find in history that "men fear freedom's
   use but love its useful name"? (See stanzas 8-12.) Do you think the
   poet was saying that having gained freedom ourselves, we now are
   unwilling to "set the dry world all ablaze with liberty"? Are we afraid
   and, if so, do we have good reason to be? Find evidence in the poem
   to support your answers.
3. In stanza 13 (lines 49-52), what contrast is made between the attitude toward freedom in Jefferson's day and our attitude toward it

today? What reason do you have for believing that MacLeish did, or did not, approve of our attitude?

4. Discuss the meaning of the concluding lines of the poem. To what does the phrase "the old stale bitter world" refer? At the time the poet was viewing it, how was it playing new? How was the "new world" of Thomas Jefferson's day playing old? State in your own words the message you think the poet intended to convey in this poem.

5. The title could refer to "the new world of the free" which Jefferson helped to create. Or it could refer to the world as the poet saw it. How do you think MacLeish intended the reader to interpret the title? Be sure that your interpretation is consistent with the tone of the poem and with the attitude of the poet.

6. Point out the ways in which this poem resembles a traditional poem in sound and structure. What qualities impress you as modern, particularly in the language?

Speech to Those Who Say Comrade

The brotherhood is not by the blood certainly:
But neither are men brothers by speech—by saying so:
Men are brothers by life lived and are hurt for it:

Hunger and hurt are the great begetters of brotherhood:
Humiliation has gotten° much love: given birth to   5
Danger I say is the nobler father and mother:

Those are as brothers whose bodies have shared fear
Or shared harm or shared hurt or indignity.
Why are the old soldiers brothers and nearest?

For this: with their minds they go over the sea a little   10
And find themselves in their youth again as they were in
Soissons and Meaux and at Ypres and those cities:

A French loaf and the girls with their eyelids painted
Bring back to aging and lonely men
Their twentieth year and the metal odor of danger: 15

It is this in life which of all things is tenderest—
To remember together with unknown men the days
Common also to them and perils ended:

It is this which makes of many a generation—
A wave of men who having the same years   20
Have in common the same dead and the changes.

The solitary and unshared experience
Dies of itself like the violations of love
Or lives on as the dead live eerily:

The unshared and single man must cover his   25
Loneliness as a girl her shame for the way of
Life is neither by one man nor by suffering.

Who are the born brothers in truth? The puddlers°   steelworkers
Scorched by the same flame in the same foundries:
Those who have spit on the same boards with the blood in it: 30

Ridden the same rivers with green logs:
Fought the police in the parks of the same cities:
Grinned for the same blows: the same flogging:

Veterans out of the same ships—factories—   35
Expeditions for fame: the founders of continents:
Those that hid in Geneva a time back:

Those that have hidden and hunted and all such—
Fought together: labored together: they carry the
Common look like a card and they pass touching.   40

Brotherhood! No word said can make you brothers!
Brotherhood only the brave earn and by danger or
Harm or by bearing hurt and by no other.

Brotherhood here in the strange world is the rich and
Rarest giving of life and the most valued: 45
Not to be had for a word or a week's wishing.

1. This poem is about the meaning of brotherhood and the people who are "born brothers in truth." How did MacLeish feel about brotherhood "here in the strange world"? What do you think he meant by "strange"? How is the world today trying to achieve brotherhood among men and nations? Do these efforts support or contradict the poet's beliefs as he expressed them in this poem?

2. What are the "great begetters of brotherhood"? In what important way are "brothers" different from other men? Why are "old soldiers brothers and nearest"? What commentary on life is brought out in lines 22-27?

3. What kind of men "carry the common look like a card"? What did MacLeish mean by this simile? What did he mean by the comment "they pass touching"?

4. In lines 42 and 43, MacLeish expressed, in a different way, the same idea conveyed in the concluding line. Do you think this is the message or theme he meant to bring out in the poem? Why did he address the poem "to those who say comrade"? Who are they? From the over-all tone of the poem, what do you think was his attitude toward them? In your opinion, does the word *speech* describe the nature and purpose of the poem? Explain.

5. In shape and sound, this poem bears a resemblance to some of Whitman's poems: the free-verse form, the three-line stanzas, and the questions answered by examples. How would you describe the effect MacLeish achieved by beginning a series of lines with a dactylic or trochaic foot, as in stanza 2? Where else in the poem do similar lines occur? Is the effect the same or different?

6. There is much concealed rhyming in this poem, particularly of end words or phrases in lines 1 and 3 of many stanzas. Point these out and discuss the nature of this ryhming.

7. Tell why you do, or do not, find this poem effective. Base your opinion on the over-all tone, and on the poet's use of metaphoric language and other poetic devices.

Marianne Moore

A consummate craftsman, Miss Moore has said of her own work, "I admit that in anything I have written, I have never achieved what satisfied me. In writing, it is my one principle that nothing is too much trouble." This principle is especially evident in her choice of words, many of them so precise that they seem inevitable. It is also evident in her descriptions, which are so imaginative and vivid that the experience, incident, or creature described almost seems to "come to life" on the page. She is, indeed, a consummate artist, distinguished particularly for her ability to convey additional or special meanings, subtly and with great charm, through unusual juxtapositions of words and images.

The form and language of Miss Moore's poems are as modern as her subjects, yet she does not hesitate to use whatever traditional techniques serve her purpose. Always her first concern is with the entire poem—the shape, sound, and emotion, as well as the meaning.

Peter[1]

Strong and slippery, built for the midnight grass-party con-
      fronted by four cats,
  he sleeps his time away—the detached first claw on the
      foreleg, which corresponds
to the thumb, retracted to its tip; the small tuft of fronds
  or katydid legs above each eye, still numbering the
      units in each group;
    the shadbones regularly set about the mouth, to
      droop or rise   5

---

[1] Peter, an actual cat, owned by friends of the poet

in unison like the porcupine's quills—motionless. He lets
      himself be flat-
  tened out by gravity, as it were a piece of seaweed tamed
      and weakened by
  exposure to the sun; compelled when extended, to lie
      stationary. Sleep is the result of his delusion that one
        must do as
      well as one can for oneself; sleep—epitome°   concise representation
      of what is to   10

him as to the average person, the end of life. Demonstrate
      on him how
  the lady caught the dangerous southern snake, placing a
      forked stick on either
  side of its innocuous° neck; one need not try to stir   harmless
      him up; his prune-shaped head and alligator eyes are
        not a party to the
      joke. Lifted and handled, he may be dangled like an
        eel or set   15

up on the forearm like a mouse; his eyes bisected by pupils
      of a pin's
  width, are flickeringly exhibited, then covered up. May
      be? I should say
  might have been; when he has been got the better of in a
      dream—as in a fight with nature or with cats—we all
        know it. Profound sleep is
      not with him a fixed illusion. Springing about with
        froglike ac-   20

curacy, emitting jerky cries when taken in the hand, he is himself
  again; to set caged by the rungs of a domestic chair would
      be unprofit-
  able—human. What is the good of hypocrisy? It
    is permissible to choose one's employment, to abandon
      the wire nail, the
      roly-poly, when it shows signs of being no longer a pleas-   25

ure, to score the adjacent magazine with a double line of
      strokes. He can
  talk, but insolently says nothing. What of it? When one
       is frank, one's very
presence is a compliment. It is clear that he can see
    the virtue of naturalness, that he is one of those who
       do not regard
       the published fact as a surrender. As for the disposition   30

invariably to affront, an animal with claws wants to have to use
  them; that eel-like extension of trunk into tail is not an
      accident. To
leap, to lengthen out, divide the air—to purloin,° to pursue. _{steal}
    To tell the hen: fly over the fence, go in the wrong
      way in your perturba-
      tion—this is life; to do less would be nothing but
      dishonesty.   .   35

1. In this poem Miss Moore is employing her usual methods for her
   usual purpose: describing with minute accuracy the appearance and
   behavior of an animal and using this to make certain observations
   about human behavior. In stanzas 1-3, what is Peter, the cat, doing?
   What particular features of the cat did the poet consider interesting
   or unusual?

2. What reason did the poet have for saying, "Maybe? I should say
   might have been"? How is this comment related to the description
   in stanzas 1-3?

3. In stanzas 5-7, what is Peter pictured as doing? What explanation
   did the poet give for his erratic behavior?

4. In stanza 6, the poet said, "It is clear that he can see the virtue of
   naturalness." Is a similar or different idea expressed in the final sentence of the poem? How do you interpret the statement in stanza 6
   that "he is one of those who do not regard the published fact as a
   surrender"?

Silence

My father used to say,
"Superior people never make long visits,
have to be shown Longfellow's grave
or the glass flowers at Harvard.
Self-reliant like the cat—   5
that takes its prey to privacy,
the mouse's limp tail hanging like a shoelace from its mouth—
they sometimes enjoy solitude,
and can be robbed of speech
by speech which has delighted them.   10
The deepest feeling always shows itself in silence;
not in silence, but restraint."
Nor was he insincere in saying, "Make my house your inn."
Inns are not residences.

1. What kind of people was the poet's father speaking about in the poem? What qualities, described in lines 2-4, distinguish them from ordinary people? What reason did he have for comparing them with a cat?

2. What is the relation between the last two lines and the rest of the poem? Do they reveal more about the father or the people? Explain.

3. The title often describes the subject of the poem or the idea conveyed in it. Tell why you do, or do not, think that such is the case in this poem.

4. The poet could have been putting words into her father's mouth that expressed her own attitude toward people, and particularly toward visitors who out-stay their welcome. In that case the tone of the poem would convey her attitude. What word, or words, do you think suggest the tone?

Critics and Connoisseurs

There is a great amount of poetry in unconscious
  fastidiousness. Certain Ming[1]
    products, imperial floor-coverings of coach-
  wheel yellow, are well enough in their way but I have
        seen something
      that I like better—a   5
        mere childish attempt to make an imperfectly
          ballasted animal stand up,
    similar determination to make a pup
      eat his meat from the plate.

I remember a swan under the willows in Oxford,
  with flamingo-colored, maple-   10
    leaflike feet. It reconnoitered like a battle-
  ship. Disbelief and conscious fastidiousness were the staple
      ingredients in its
        disinclination to move. Finally its hardihood was not
          proof against its
        proclivity° to more fully appraise such bits   inclination 15
        of food as the stream

bore counter to it; it made away with which I gave it
  to eat. I have seen this swan and
  I have seen you; I have seen ambition without
  understanding in a variety of forms. Happening to stand   20
    by an ant-hill, I have
      seen a fastidious ant carrying a stick north, south, east,
        west, till it turned on
      itself, struck out from the flower-bed into the lawn,
        and returned to the point

---

[1] Ming. Many products of the Ming dynasty (1368-1644) were elaborately deco-
rated with much attention to details.

from which it had started. Then abandoning the stick as   25
  useless and overtaxing its
    jaws with a particle of whitewash—pill-like but
  heavy, it again went through the same course of procedure.
          What is
      there in being able
        to say that one has dominated the stream in an   30
            attitude of self-defence;
          in proving that one has had the experience
            of carrying a stick?

1. What likeness did the poet see between the ancient Ming products and the attempts of the child? What do these have in common with poetry?
2. What impression did the poet create of the swan and the ant? What choices did they make? What determined their choices? Do you think that the poet was suggesting that the behavior of these creatures illustrates the "ambition without understanding" which she had observed in people? What do you think she meant by the question she asked at the end of the poem?
3. The title would suggest that the purpose of the poem is to comment on those people whose profession or hobby is to make critical judgments. Do you think the swan represents the critic and the ant the connoisseur or *vice versa?* Give reasons for your answer. In your opinion, what comment was the poet making about critics and connoisseurs? What was her attitude toward them? Where in the poem is this revealed?
4. When the poet was merely recounting what she had observed, she used rather simple, direct language. What word, or words, would you use to describe the language she used when *commenting* on her observations? How did this change in language affect the tone and meaning of the poem?

The Icosasphere

"In Buckinghamshire hedgerows
   the birds nesting in the merged green density,
      weave little bits of string and moths and feathers and
         thistledown,
         in parabolic concentric curves"
and, working for concavity, leave spherical feats of rare   5
         efficiency;
   whereas through lack of integration,

avid for someone's fortune,[1]
   three were slain and ten committed perjury,
      six died, two killed themselves, and two paid fines for
         risks they'd run.
      But then there is the icosasphere   10
in which at last we have steel-cutting at its summit of
         economy,
      since twenty triangles conjoined, can wrap one

ball or double-rounded shell
   with almost no waste, so geometrically
      neat, it's an icosahedron. Would the engineers making one,   15
      or Mr. J. O. Jackson[2] tell us
   how the Egyptians could have set up seventy-eight-foot
         solid granite vertically?
   We should like to know how that was done.

---

[1] *someone's fortune*, the $30,000,000 snuff fortune of Mrs. H. E. S. Garrett, who died without children or a will. More than 25,900 people made claims to the fortune.

[2] *Mr. J. O. Jackson*, inventor of the icosasphere, a design for a steel sphere made of twenty equilateral triangles, hence economical to cut

1. What does the icosasphere represent? How do you think that the poet felt about it? Why did it remind her of the birds in Buckingham

hedgerows and the Egyptians who built the pyramids? Why do you think she included the reference to the fortune seekers?

2. The tone of the poem might suggest that the poet was poking fun at people who are overly impressed by modern technology. What clues are you given in the poem that do, or do not, support such a conclusion?

3. In your opinion, does the combination of technical terms and colloquial language contribute to the over-all effect of the poem? If so, why?

To a Steam Roller

The illustration
is nothing to you without the application.
    You lack half wit. You crush all the particles down
        into close conformity, and then walk back and forth
            on them.

Sparkling chips of rock   5
are crushed down to the level of the parent block.
    Were not "impersonal judgment in aesthetic°   pertaining to beauty
        matters, a metaphysical° impossibility," you   absolute

might fairly achieve
it. As for butterflies, I can hardly conceive   10
    of one's attending upon you, but to question
        the congruence of the complement is vain, if it exists.

1. What did the steam roller do that demonstrated a lack of sensitivity? Why might this permit the steam roller to achieve "impersonal judgment in aesthetic matters"? Why was the steam roller called half witted?

2. If a butterfly should attend a steam roller, would the steam roller be likely to consider it congruous or incongruous? What would the poet think of the congruence? In what way could you say a butterfly was an illustration without being applied to anything? Do you know anybody who resembles the steam roller? What do they always insist on doing with your illustrations?

The Monkey Puzzle[1]

A kind of monkey or pine-lemur
not of interest to the monkey
in a kind of Flaubert's Carthage, it defies one—
this "Paduan cat with lizard," this "tiger in a bamboo thicket."
"An interwoven somewhat," it will not come out.   5
Ignore the Foo dog and it is forthwith more than a dog,
its tail superimposed upon itself in a complacent half spiral,
incidentally so witty;
but this pine-tree—this pine-tiger, is a tiger, not a dog.
It knows that if a nomad may have dignity,   10
Gibraltar has had more—
that "it is better to be lonely than unhappy."
A conifer contrived in imitation of the glyptic[2] work of jade
    and hard-stone cutters,
a true curio in this bypath of curio collecting,
it is worth its weight in gold, but no one takes it   15
from these woods in which society's not knowing is colossal,
the lion's ferocious chrysanthemum head seeming kind by
    comparison.
This porcupine-quilled, complicated starkness—
this is beauty—"a certain proportion in the skeleton which
    gives the best results."
One is at a loss, however, to know why it should be here,   20
in this morose part of the earth—
to account for its origin at all;
but we prove, we do not explain our birth.

---

[1] monkey puzzle, a striking, intricately shaped evergreen tree native to Chile, occasionally seen in parks or estate gardens
[2] glyptic, carving in hard stone

1. On a first reading, this poem seems as much of a puzzle as the
   strange tree called the monkey puzzle. Why did the poet say of it,
   "it defies one" (line 3) and, later, "it will not come out" (line 5)?

2. The poet made several attempts to describe the tree's appearance. Point these out and indicate what characteristics of the tree each suggests. Does this kind of tree have any value? To whom? What clues can you find to indicate (1) the nature of the tree's place of origin, and (2) the poet's feeling toward the tree?

3. Lines 20-23 provide a kind of conclusion based on the poet's attempt to make sense of this natural phenomenon. How do you interpret them, particularly the last line?

Four Quartz Crystal Clocks

There are four vibrators, the world's exactest clocks;
   and these quartz time-pieces that tell
time intervals to other clocks,
   these worksless clocks work well;
independently the same, kept in   5
   the 41°[1] Bell
      Laboratory time

vault. Checked by a comparator with Arlington,
   they punctualize the "radio,
cinema," and "presse,"—a group the   10
   Giraudoux[2] truth-bureau
of hoped-for accuracy has termed
   "instruments of truth." We know—
      as Jean Giraudoux says

certain Arabs have not heard—that Napoleon   15
   is dead; that a quartz prism when
the temperature changes, feels
   the change and that the then
electrified alternate edges
   oppositely charged, threaten   20
      careful timing; so that

[1] 41°. The laboratory time vault is kept at 41°.
[2] Giraudoux, skeptical French playwright

this water-clear crystal as the Greeks used to say,
 this "clear ice" must be kept at the
same coolness. Repetition, with
 the scientist, should be   25
synonymous with accuracy.
 The lemur-student can see
  that an aye-aye is not

an angwan-tíbo, potto, or loris.[3] The sea-
 side burden should not embarrass   30
the bell-boy with the buoy-ball
 endeavoring to pass
hotel patronesses; nor could a
 practised ear confuse the glass
  eyes for taxidermists   35

with eye-glasses from the optometrist. And as
 MEridian-7 one-two
one-two[4] gives, each fifteenth second
 in the same voice, the new
data—"The time will be" so and so—   40
 you realize that "when you
  hear the signal," you'll be

hearing Jupiter or jour pater, the day god—
 the salvaged son of Father Time—
telling the cannibal Chronos[5]   45
 (eater of his proxime
newborn progeny) that punctuality
 is not a crime.

---

[3] aye-aye . . . loris, varieties of lemur—a monkey-like animal
[4] MEridian-7 . . . one-two, number to call for correct time
[5] Chronos, in classical mythology, a giant who devoured
 all his children except Jupiter, Neptune, and Pluto

1. Why are the four crystal clocks kept in a laboratory time vault?
What function do the clocks perform? Why are "radio," "cinema,"
and the "presse" termed "instruments of truth"?

2. In stanza 4 the poet stated a general principle: "Repetition should be synonymous with accuracy." How is this idea related to the four clocks? In the following stanzas, what did the poet suggest might happen if we were to rely solely on repetition for accuracy?

3. Although the poem seems to be about clocks and time, its purpose might be to explore the idea of what truth is. What kind of truth do you think is represented (1) by the four clocks, (2) by the lemur-student, and (3) by Jupiter?

4. Find examples of rhyme and a play-on-words which add amusement to the poem. In what way do they supply a clue to the tone of the poem? By what means does the poet weave the stanzas closely together?

E. E. Cummings

For many readers, the verse of E. E. Cummings exemplifies modern poetry. It is unique, experimental, sometimes difficult, and almost always flippant. His eccentric capitalization and punctuation—the most striking features of his work—have been widely imitated by self-styled disciples. His experiments with words—sometimes cutting them apart or joining them together, sometimes arranging them in unusual patterns on the printed page—have influenced the work of many later poets. His experiments have not, however, been limited solely to typography. They include the effects achieved through words and combinations of words. The syntax of his sentences is also eccentric. Words which commonly function as one part of speech are assigned the duties of another part, as in "a perhaps hand." At times, the punctuation serves more to emphasize key words and phrases than to indicate sentence structure.

To readers of all ages, Cummings' poetry has a special appeal. Whether he was writing about love, the coming of spring, or the death of Buffalo Bill, he was witty, ironic and, frequently, satirical.

Buffalo Bill's

Buffalo Bill's
defunct
    who used to
    ride a watersmooth-silver
                stallion   5
and break onetwothreefourfive pigeonsjustlikethat
                              Jesus

he was a handsome man
                    and what i want to know is
how do you like your blueeyed boy   10
Mister Death

1. The language of this poem is as unconventional as its shape. What kind of person do you think might speak this way? How does this person feel toward Buffalo Bill? To whom is he speaking and why? What is the tone of the poem?

2. The poet arranged each word, or group of words, in order to achieve a particular effect. Why do you think he set certain words, like *defunct* and *stallion*, off by themselves, and ran others together, as in line 6? Notice what happens when you read lines 1-6 as though it were written as a single sentence.

3. In line 2, the poet could have used *dead* instead of *defunct*. Why do you think he chose *defunct*?

Spring is like a perhaps hand

Spring is like a perhaps hand
(which comes carefully
out of Nowhere)arranging
a window, into which people look (while
people stare   5
arranging and changing placing
carefully there a strange
thing and a known thing here)and

changing everything carefully

spring is like a perhaps   10
Hand in a window
(carefully to
and fro moving New and
Old things,while
people stare carefully   15
moving a perhaps
fraction of flower here placing
an inch of air there)and

without breaking anything.

1. Why do you think that spring reminded the poet of the "perhaps
   hand" of a window dresser? What is suggested by the phrase
   "perhaps hand"? In your opinion, why did the poet choose this
   phrase to describe the coming of spring?
2. In lines 6-9 and again in lines 16-19, the poet described things being
   done. In each case, who was doing them—spring, the window dresser,
   the people, or both?
3. Why do you think the poet placed line 9 and the last line by themselves? Why is the last line particularly important to the meaning
   of the poem? What is the mood of the poem?

4. Point out examples of Cummings' eccentric capitalization, punctuation, and syntax. In your opinion, do they add to your enjoyment of the poem or detract from it? Explain why.

what if a much of a which of a wind

what if a much of a which of a wind
gives the truth to summer's lie;
bloodies with dizzying leaves the sun
and yanks immortal stars awry?
Blow king to beggar and queen to seem   5
(blow friend to fiend:blow space to time)
—when skies are hanged and oceans drowned,
the single secret will still be man

what if a keen of a lean wind flays
screaming hills with sleet and snow: 10
strangles valleys by ropes of thing
and stifles forests in white ago?
Blow hope to terror;blow seeing to blind
(blow pity to envy and soul to mind)
—whose hearts are mountains,roots are trees,   15
it's they shall cry hello to the spring

what if a dawn of a doom of a dream
bites this universe in two,
peels forever out of his grave
and sprinkles nowhere with me and you?   20
Blow soon to never and never to twice
(blow life to isn't:blow death to was)
—all nothing's only our hugest home;
the most who die,the more we live

The impression you probably gained from a first reading of this poem is that the poet was experimenting with the sounds of words. As you re-read the lines aloud, listen for the alliteration, the repetition of certain consonant sounds, internal rhyme, and end rhyme. Point out examples of each which you found particularly effective.

2. Discovering the meaning of the poem may require several re-readings. Note that the poem is in the form of a dialogue; each stanza contains a question and an answer. What events are described and what questions asked in the first four lines of each stanza? Note that each "answer" (the last four lines of each stanza) is divided into two parts which are separated by a dash. What is the function of each of these parts? What theme, or general truth, is expressed in the final couplet in each stanza?

3. Chart the rhythm of the first stanza. Do the other stanzas follow a similar or different pattern? If there is a predominant rhythm, see if you can identify it and the metrical foot or feet which create this rhythm.

4. Cummings chose words that were not only *exact*; they were also surprising. Note, for example, the word *yanks* in line 4 and the words *hanged* and *drowned* in line 7. Find others equally surprising and tell why you do, or do not, consider them effective.

5. What device did the poet use in each stanza in the pair of lines which follow each opening question? Why do you think he used this device? Can you see any reason for the parentheses around the second line in each pair? Discuss.

pity this busy monster,manunkind

pity this busy monster,manunkind,

not. Progress is a comfortable disease:
your victim(death and life safely beyond)

plays with the bigness of his littleness
—electrons deify one razorblade   5
into a mountainrange;lenses extend

unwish through curving wherewhen till unwish
returns on its unself.

A world of made
is not a world of born—pity poor flesh   10

and trees,poor stars and stones,but never this
fine specimen of hypermagical

ultraomnipotence. We doctors know

a hopeless case if—listen:there's a hell
of a good universe next door;let's go

1. Cummings, like Ogden Nash, didn't hesitate to invent words to create a particular effect. What is this "busy monster" which he called "manunkind"? Why doesn't it deserve pity? What should be pitied?

2. Who is "your victim" described in lines 3 and 4? What is the matter with him? Why is his case called "hopeless" (line 14)?

3. What criticism of modern man is implied in lines 4-8? State in your own words what you think the poet meant by "A world of made is not a world of born." How do you interpret the last statement in the poem beginning "We doctors know . . ."?

4. Here, as in most of Cummings' poems, every unusual word, or arrangement of words, affects both the meaning and the over-all tone. Point out examples of these and state what meaning and tone you think the poet intended.

Wallace Stevens

Wallace Stevens was truly a "self-made" poet. By vocation an insurance executive, he did not reach the peak of his creative powers until after he was fifty. Neither did he have much contact with other poets, which may explain why he never became identified with a particular group. He described himself as one who "still dwells in an ivory tower, but who insists that life there would be intolerable except for the fact that one has, from the top, such an exceptional view of the public dump and the advertising signs . . ." He did not like what he saw, but he did not dedicate his talent either to condemning it (except indirectly) or to proposing a new order of society. His concern was with the interplay between reality and imagination, and with what the creative use of imagination could make of reality. Man, he believed, must find his redemption not through rebellion or blind faith but rather through the discovery of beauty in the commonplace.

Some of Stevens' poems are bizarrely imaginative; most of them might be described as "useless" in that they offer the reader no advice and no consolation. Each has its own artistry and purpose. Each seems to come effortlessly from the poet's pen, full of color, sound, and imagery—and rich in meaning.

Another Weeping Woman

Pour the unhappiness out
From your too bitter heart,
Which grieving will not sweeten.

Poison grows in this dark.
It is in the water of tears   5
Its black blooms rise.

The magnificent cause of being,
The imagination, the one reality
In this imagined world

Leaves you   10
With him for whom no phantasy moves,
And you are pierced by a death.

1. Why did the poet believe that the woman would find no comfort in
   grieving? Why was she weeping? What warning is expressed in the
   metaphor and its development in stanza 2? To what does the word
   poison refer?
2. In stanza 3, the poet suggested a reason for the woman's bitterness.
   What "cause of being" has left her with the one for whom she
   grieves? In what "imagined world" is this cause the "one reality"?
3. Note the unusual use of the verb *pierced* in the last line. What
   relation do you see between it and verbs *pour* (line 1) and *leaves*
   (line 10)? What image do they create in the mind?
4. To intensify the effect of the poem, Stevens used several poetic
   devices. Note, for example, lines 1, 4, and 10, and lines 2 and 6.
   Identify these devices and discuss the kind of effect they create.

The Woman in Sunshine

It is only that this warmth and movement are like
The warmth and movement of a woman.

It is not that there is any image in the air
Nor the beginning nor end of a form:

It is empty. But a woman in threadless gold   5
Burns us with brushings of her dress

And a dissociated abundance of being,
More definite for what she is—

Because she is disembodied,
Bearing the odors of the summer fields,   10

Confessing the taciturn° and yet indifferent,   habitually silent
Invisibly clear, the only love.

1. This poem is built on an implied comparison—a metaphor. To what
   did the poet compare sunshine? (Note the title.) What qualities
   common to both are brought out through the metaphor? What did
   the poet mean by the statement, "It is empty"? To what does *it* refer?
2. Does the woman of the title have a physicial reality? Why did he
   say that she was "more definite for what she is"?
3. In the last two stanzas, what other qualities of the sunshine are
   brought out through the metaphor? State in your own words what you
   think the poet meant by "confessing the taciturn" and "the only love"?

The Snow Man

One must have a mind of winter
To regard the frost and the boughs
Of the pine-trees crusted with snow;

And have been cold a long time
To behold the junipers shagged with ice,   5
The spruces rough in the distant glitter

Of the January sun; and not to think
Of any misery in the sound of the wind,
In the sound of a few leaves,

Which is the sound of the land   10
Full of the same wind
That is blowing in the same bare place

For the listener, who listens in the snow,
And, nothing himself, beholds
Nothing that is not there and the nothing that is.   15

1. Is the listener also the "snow man" of the title? Note that snow and man are written separately rather than as snowman. On the basis of what is said in the poem, how do you interpret the title?

2. If a person is to view the winter beauty, what must he bring to the experience? What must he not think about as he listens to the wind? Why not?

3. State in your own words what you think the poet meant in the last two lines. What relation do you see between the "one" in line 1 and the listener in line 13?

4. Note that the entire poem is a single sentence. As you read the poem again, try to discover whether or not this has any effect on the tone or over-all impression of the poem. Listen for words and repetition of words which contribute to the sound of the poem.

Martial Cadenza

Only this evening I saw again low in the sky
The evening star, at the beginning of winter, the star
That in spring will crown every western horizon,
Again . . . as if it came back, as if life came back,
Not in a later son, a different daughter, another place,   5
But as if evening found us young, still young,
Still walking in a present of our own.

It was like sudden time in a world without time,
This world, this place, the street in which I was,
Without time: as that which is not has no time,   10
Is not, or is of what there was, is full
Of the silence before the armies, armies without
Either trumpets or drums, the commanders mute, the arms
On the ground, fixed fast in a profound defeat.

What had this star to do with the world it lit,   15
With the blank skies over England, over France
And above the German camps? It looked apart.
Yet it is this that shall maintain—Itself
Is time, apart from any past, apart
From any future, the ever-living and being,   20
The ever-breathing and moving, the constant fire,

The present close, the present realized,
Not the symbol but that for which the symbol stands,
The vivid thing in the air that never changes,
Though the air change. Only this evening I saw it again,   25
At the beginning of winter, and I walked and talked
Again, and lived and was again, and breathed again
And moved again and flashed again, time flashed again.

1. In stanza 1, exactly what did the poet see? What was there about the sight that led him to think about time?

2. In stanza 2, how did his feelings about the world around him change as a result of his experience? What difference did he sense between what the star represents and what the war represents (stanzas 2 and 3)? How did his new vision affect his feeling about life?

3. Why do you think the poet returned again in stanza 4 to the experience of seeing the star? Was it to dispel the uncertainty expressed in lines 4-7? Is the mood of these closing lines the same as that of the entire poem, or is it different? Explain.

4. Throughout the poem the poet used repetition to create a particular effect, sometimes to sharpen the meaning or to enrich the sound. Find examples of the repetition of words and phrases which create an interplay of sound. Discuss their effect.

No Possum, No Sop, No Taters[1]

He is not here, the old sun,
As absent as if we were asleep.

The field is frozen. The leaves are dry.
Bad is final in this light.

In this bleak air the broken stalks   5
Have arms without hands. They have trunks

Without legs or, for that, without heads.
They have heads in which a captive cry

Is merely the moving of a tongue.
Snow sparkles like eyesight falling to earth,   10

Like seeing fallen brightly away.
The leaves hop, scraping on the ground.

———
[1] No . . . taters, Southern saying for utter destitution

It is deep January. The sky is hard.
The stalks are firmly rooted in ice.

It is in this solitude, a syllable,   15
Out of these gawky flitterings,

Intones its single emptiness,
The savagest hollow of winter-sound.

It is here, in this bad, that we reach
The last purity of the knowledge of good.   20

The crow looks rusty as he rises up.
Bright is the malice in his eye . . .

One joins him there for company,
But at a distance, in another tree.

1. Why did the poet refer to this winter scene as "bad," first in line 4
    and again in line 19? What did he mean by the statement in stanza
    1? How is this related to the statement in line 4?
2. What impressions of hopelessness are conveyed by the images describ-
    ing the stalks, the snow, and the leaves? Which of these images did
    you find particularly effective?
3. The over-all effect of the scene was one of desolation. What words
    and phrases in lines 15-18 convey this feeling?
4. How do you interpret the last three stanzas? What do you think the
    poet meant by "the last purity of the knowledge of good"? How
    does the crow fit into the picture of the bad? Why would one join
    him for company, but at a distance?
5. What do you think is the purpose of the poem? What is the mood?
    In your opinion, do the two-line stanzas and the many short sentences
    help to create the mood? Discuss.

W. H. Auden

Unlike many modern poets, Auden has been as concerned with examining social and political problems in his poetry as with expressing personal emotions. This concern is reflected in some of the subjects he has chosen to write about, particularly in the 1930's and 1940's; namely, war, the corruption of modern society, and the dichotomy between the rich and the poor.

Like Eliot, he has employed a wide variety of forms and styles, from free verse to the alliterative verse of the Middle Ages. Although his use of words is always precise, it is sometimes unorthodox. Occasionally he even omits words customarily included in conventional sentence structures. This verbal compression, however much it may challenge the general reader, lends a special quality of compactness and intensity to Auden's best poems.

The Unknown Citizen

(To JS/07/M/378 This Marble Monument Is Erected by the State)

He was found by the Bureau of Statistics to be
One against whom there was no official complaint,
And all the reports on his conduct agree
That, in the modern sense of an old-fashioned word, he was a
    saint,
For in everything he did he served the Greater Community.   5
Except for the War till the day he retired
He worked in a factory and never got fired,
But satisfied his employers, Fudge Motors Inc.

Yet he wasn't a scab° or odd in his views,   non-union worker
For his Union reports that he paid his dues,   10
(Our report on his Union shows it was sound)
And our Social Psychology workers found
That he was popular with his mates and liked a drink.
The Press are convinced that he bought a paper every day
And that his reactions to advertisements were normal in every
    way.   15
Policies taken out in his name prove that he was fully insured,
And his Health-card shows he was once in hospital but left it
    cured.
Both Producers Research and High-Grade Living declare
He was fully sensible to the advantages of the Installment Plan
And had everything necessary to the Modern Man,   20
A phonograph, a radio, a car and a frigidaire.
Our researchers into Public Opinion are content
That he held the proper opinions for the time of year;
When there was peace, he was for peace; when there was
    war, he went.
He was married and added five children to the population,   25
Which our Eugenist says was the right number for a parent
    of his generation,
And our teachers report that he never interfered with their
    education.
Was he free? Was he happy? The question is absurd:
Had anything been wrong, we should certainly have heard.

1. What kind of person was the man described in this poem? What was
   the poet's attitude toward him? At what point in your reading did
   you become aware of this attitude?
2. How would you explain the title and the peculiar dedication of the
   poem? What word or words would you use to describe the over-all
   tone of the poem: ironic, satiric, tragic, comic? Support your answer
   with specific references to the poem. Be sure to account for the last
   two lines.

O Where Are You Going?

"O where are you going?" said reader to rider,
"That valley is fatal when furnaces burn,
Yonder's the midden° whose odors will madden,   heap of refuse
That gap is the grave where the tall return."

"O do you imagine," said fearer to farer,°   traveler   5
"That dusk will delay on your path to the pass,
Your diligent looking discover the lacking
Your footsteps feel from granite to grass?"

"O what was that bird," said horror to hearer,
"Did you see that shape in the twisted trees?   10
Behind you swiftly the figure comes softly,
The spot on your skin is a shocking disease."

"Out of this house"—said rider to reader,
"Yours never will"—said farer to fearer,
"They're looking for you"—said hearer to horror,   15
As he left them there, as he left them there.

1. This poem resembles an allegory in that it tells a story in which people
   or happenings have another meaning. Who are the speakers in stanzas
   1-3? What kind of people do they represent? What do you think is
   the purpose of their questions?

2. What kind of people are represented by the rider, farer, and hearer?
   How did they react to the speakers? Relate the answers in stanza 4 to
   the questions in stanzas 1-3. What attitudes do these answers convey?
   How do you interpret the last line?

3. Do you think that the questioners and the answerers represent (1) different kinds of people in the world or (2) the different ways in which
   a single individual looks at the experiences of life? What truth or
   observation do you think the poet meant to express allegorically in this
   poem? Base your answer on a careful study of the poem.

4. Where in the poem did the poet use alliteration as part of the structure? Find other examples of its use. In your opinion, was the alliteration important to the effect achieved in the poem? Explain as best you can.

Under Sirius[1]

Yes, these are the dog-days,° Fortunatus:	hot, humid days
The heather lies limp and dead	
On the mountain, the baltering° torrent	tumbling
Shrunk to a soodling thread;	
Rusty the spears of the legion, unshaven its captain,	5
Vacant the scholar's brain	
Under his great hat,	
Drug as she may the Sibyl utters	
A gush of table-chat.	
And you yourself with a head-cold and upset stomach,	10
Lying in bed till noon,	
Your bills unpaid, your much advertised	
Epic not yet begun,	
Are a sufferer too. All day, you tell us, you wish	
Some earthquake would astonish	15
Or the wind of the Comforter's wing	
Unlock the prisons and translate°	transform
The slipshod gathering.	
And last night, you say, you dreamed of that bright blue	
morning,	
The hawthorn hedges in bloom,	20
When, serene in their ivory vessels,	
The three wise Maries[1] come,	
Sossing° through seamless waters, piloted in	moving gently
By sea-horse and fluent dolphin:	

---

[1] Sirius, the dog star

[1] three ... Maries, the Virgin Mary, Mary Magdalene, and Mary the mother of James

Ah! how the cannons roar,   25
How jocular the bells as They
Indulge the peccant° shore.   sinful

It is natural to hope and pious, of course, to believe
    That all in the end shall be well,
But first of all, remember,   30
    So the Sacred Books foretell,
The rotten fruit shall be shaken. Would your hope make sense
    If today were that moment of silence
    Before it break and drown
When the insurrected eagre° hangs   tidal wave   35
    Over the sleeping town?

How will you look and what will you do when the basalt
    Tombs of the sorcerers shatter
And their guardian megalopods°   giant-footed creatures
    Come after you pitter-patter?   40
How will you answer when from their qualming° spring   doubt-
    The immortal nymphs fly shrieking   producing
    And out of the open sky
The pantocratic° riddle breaks—   all-ruling
    "Who are you and why?"   45

For when in a carol° under the apple-trees   ring-dance
    The reborn featly° dance,   nimbly
There will also, Fortunatus,
    Be those who refused their chance,
Now pottering shades, querulous° beside the salt-pits,   complaining 50
    And mawkish° in their wits,   sentimental
    To whom these dull dog-days
Between event seem crowned with olive
    And golden with self-praise.

1. To the Greeks and Romans the rising of the star Sirius was a token of
    summer heat. In the first stanza, the speaker in the poem pictured the
    general effect of being under the influence of Sirius. Describe the
    particular effect on Fortunatus. What would he like to see happen?

What did he dream as taking place? How did the speaker react? (See stanza 4.) How do you interpret his question beginning "Would your hope . . ." (line 33)?

2. The changes which Fortunatus wished for could bring about unexpected results. What are these? How do you interpret stanza 5? What reason can you give for thinking that the speaker did, or did not, expect an answer?

3. The satiric tone of the poem results in part from Auden's having combined classical allusions with modern colloquial language. The Sibyl, for example, was a mythological fortune teller who uttered profound truths while under the influence of divine drugs; yet, in the poem, she engages in "table-chat." Find other examples of this comic device and show what they contribute to the over-all tone of the poem.

Richard Wilbur

Despite Richard Wilbur's youth (he is the youngest poet represented in this collection), he has already published four volumes of first-rate verse. Though clearly influenced by such poets as Emily Dickinson and Marianne Moore, he has developed a style quite his own. His verse, often characterized by a conversational quality, is lyrical and graceful. His rhyme is never over-worked or over-emphatic.

The wit, the play of word and image, and the rigorous structure in Wilbur's poems can be deceptive. His work is ultimately neither artificial nor formalistic, but reveals his profound understanding of the rapid changes and cross-currents of modern life.

Juggler

A ball will bounce, but less and less. It's not
A light-hearted thing, resents its own resilience.
Falling is what it loves, and the earth falls
So in our hearts from brilliance,
Settles and is forgot.   5
It takes a skyblue juggler with five red balls

To shake our gravity up. Whee, in the air
The balls roll round, wheel on his wheeling hands,
Learning the ways of lightness, alter to spheres
Grazing his finger ends,   10
Cling to their courses there,
Swinging a small heaven about his ears.

But a heaven is easier made of nothing at all
Than the earth regained, and still and sole within
The spin of worlds, with a gesture sure and noble   15
He reels that heaven in,
Landing it ball by ball,
And trades it all for a broom, a plate, a table.

Oh, on his toe the table is turning, the broom's
Balancing up on his nose, and the plate whirls   20
On the tip of the broom! Damn, what a show, we cry:
The boys stamp, and the girls
Shriek, and the drum booms
And all comes down, and he bows and says good-bye.

If the juggler is tired now, if the broom stands   25
In the dust again, if the table starts to drop
Through the daily dark again, and though the plate
Lies flat on the table top,
For him we batter our hands
Who has won for once over the world's weight.   30

1. Why do "we batter our hands" for the juggler? In what way are the
   ball and the earth alike? How do you interpret lines 3-7?

2. In stanzas 2 and 3, the poet extended the comparison introduced in
   stanza 1. What is suggested in lines 11 and 12? What did the poet
   mean by "a heaven is easier made of nothing at all than the earth
   regained"?

3. Why do you think he described the juggler's tricks with a broom, a
   plate, and a table? What did they prove? Was it the same as what was
   proved by the juggling of the balls? What explanation can you give for
   the wild enthusiasm of the audience?

4. Some of the lines of the poem consist of a single phrase or clause;
   others consist of two or more. What effect do you think the poet
   intended to create? Was he trying to convey through the sound of the
   poem much the same impression as is conveyed in the word-pictures?
   Explain.

5. What words did you find especially effective in conveying the exact
   meaning, image, or sensory impression?

Museum Piece

The good grey guardians of art
Patrol the halls on spongy shoes,
Impartially protective, though
Perhaps suspicious of Toulouse.

Here dozes one against the wall,   5
Disposed upon a funeral chair.
A Degas dancer pirouettes
Upon the parting of his hair.

See how she spins! The grace is there,
But strain as well is plain to see.   10
Degas loved the two together:
Beauty joined to energy.

Edgar Degas purchased once
A fine El Greco, which he kept
Against the wall beside his bed   15
To hang his pants on while he slept.

1. A visit to a museum would seem a more suitable subject for a serious
   poem than for a humorous poem. What did the poet find amusing
   about the guards and the picture of the dancer? Was the anecdote
   about Degas amusing in the same way? Is incongruity often a source
   of humor? Discuss.
2. What reason do you have for believing that the poet appreciated the
   beautiful as well as the amusing? What purpose do you think he had
   in mind when he wrote this poem?
3. Discuss the imagery and the words which create it. How important are
   they to the charm and humor of the poem?

Still, Citizen Sparrow

Still, citizen sparrow, this vulture which you call
Unnatural, let him but lumber again to air
Over the rotten office, let him bear
The carrion° ballast up, and at the tall   flesh of
                                                         a carcass

Tip of the sky lie cruising. Then you'll see   5
That no more beautiful bird is in heaven's height,
No wider more placid wings, no watchfuller flight;
He shoulders nature there, the frightfully free,

The naked-headed one. Pardon him, you
Who dart in the orchard aisles, for it is he   10
Devours death, mocks mutability,°   changeability
Has heart to make an end, keeps nature new.

Thinking of Noah, childheart, try to forget
How for so many bedlam hours his saw
Soured the song of birds with its wheezy gnaw,   15
And the slam of his hammer all the day beset

The people's ears. Forget that he could bear
To see the towns like coral under the keel,
And the fields so dismal deep. Try rather to feel
How high and weary it was, on the waters where   20

He rocked his only world, and everyone's.
Forgive the hero, you who would have died
Gladly with all you knew; he rode that tide
To Ararat; all men are Noah's sons.

1. What kind of person is represented by "citizen sparrow"? Why do
you think the poet made such a point about the vulture? What had
the sparrow not understood or failed to observe? Why should the
sparrow pardon the vulture rather than condemn him?

2. As the poet spoke of the vulture, why was he reminded of Noah and the ark? What did he ask the sparrow to forget about Noah for which Noah could have been condemned? What did the poet ask the sparrow to try to feel? Why was Noah a hero whom the sparrow should forgive?

3. The tone of the poem is that of a conversation between a gentle and wise person and a child. (Note the reference to the sparrow as "child-heart.") Why does the world need vultures as well as sparrows? What truth about life and people was the poet bringing out in his defense of the vulture and of Noah? How do you interpret the poet's final comment, "all men are Noah's sons"?

4. The language and subject of this poem are unquestionably modern, yet in giving them form the poet used the traditional four-line stanza and rhyme. What is the rhyme scheme? Does the poem also have a predominant rhythm pattern?

Year's-End

Now winter downs the dying of the year,
And night is all a settlement of snow;
From the soft street the rooms of houses show
A gathered light, a shapen atmosphere,
Like frozen-over lakes whose ice is thin   5
And still allows some stirring down within.

I've known the wind by water banks to shake
The late leaves down, which frozen where they fell
And held in ice as dancers in a spell
Fluttered all winter long into a lake;   10
Graved° on the dark in gestures of descent,   *engraved*
They seemed their own most perfect monument.

There was perfection in the death of ferns
Which laid their fragile cheeks against the stone
A million years. Great mammoths overthrown   15
Composedly have made their long sojourns,
Like palaces of patience, in the gray
And changeless lands of ice. And at Pompeii

The little dog lay curled and did not rise
But slept the deeper as the ashes rose   20
And found the people incomplete, and froze
The random hands, the loose unready eyes
Of men expecting yet another sun
To do the shapely thing they had not done.

These sudden ends of time must give us pause.   25
We fray into the future, rarely wrought
Save in the tapestries of afterthought.
More time, more time. Barrages of applause
Come muffled from a buried radio.
The New-year bells are wrangling with the snow.   30

1. As the poet thought about the dying of the year, what winter scenes
   did he recall? What impression is conveyed in stanza 1 through the
   simile (line 5)?
2. In stanza 2, why did the poet consider the ice-bound leaves "their
   own most perfect monument"? With what did he compare the leaves?
   Why was the resulting image effective?
3. To what "ends of time" was the poet referring in stanzas 3 and 4?
   What words help you to picture the death of ferns and the movements of the great mammoths? Why was the eruption of the volcano
   at Pompeii also an end of time? What words and phrases convey the
   tragic consequences?
4. In the closing lines the poet recalls the celebrations with which people
   greet the "year's end." Why do you think he referred to the applause
   as a "barrage" and to the radio as "buried"? What connection can you
   see between the radio and the other victims of time mentioned in the
   preceding stanzas?
5. In the images in lines 26 and 27, do you think the poet was implying
   that we can never know what lies ahead and that only when we are
   able to look back can we discover a pattern and meaning? Or is he
   suggesting that it is foolish to think of time in terms of single years?
   What did he mean by "more time, more time"? Do you think he felt
   we could learn by being aware of the "sudden ends of time?" If so,
   what could we learn? Each of you may interpret the last stanza in a
   different way and thus arrive at different meanings. Few poems—
   especially modern poems—have a single meaning—seldom an obvious
   one.

The Beautiful Changes

One wading a Fall meadow finds on all sides
The Queen Anne's Lace lying like lilies
On water; it glides
So from the walker, it turns
Dry grass to a lake, as the slightest shade of you   5
Valleys my mind in fabulous blue Lucernes.[1]

The beautiful changes as a forest is changed
By a chameleon's tuning his skin to it;
As a mantis, arranged
On a green leaf, grows   10
Into it, makes the leaf leafier, and proves
Any greenness is deeper than anyone knows.

Your hands hold roses always in a way that says
They are not only yours; the beautiful changes
In such kind ways,   15
Wishing ever to sunder
Things and things' selves for a second finding, to lose
For a moment all that it touches back to wonder.

---

[1] Lucernes, reference to Lake of Lucerne, Switzerland

1. The "beautiful" described in each stanza seems to undergo a change
   as the viewer observes it, or to bring about a change. How do you
   account for this seeming change? Is it in the mind of the viewer? Is it
   due to his feelings toward another person? Is it due to some unusual
   relationship between things; for example, the mantis on the leaf?
   Which, if any, of these explanations are suggested in the last stanza?
2. What picture is presented in stanza 1 through the two similes? What
   is being compared in each simile?
3. Stanza 2 also contains two similes. What are they? What kind of
   change is suggested in the forest? What did the viewer mean by his
   comment about the mantis (lines 10-12)?

4. The phrase "second finding" (stanza 3) might suggest the kind of change which the viewer observed in the field and in the forest. What would you say this "second finding" is? What words in this stanza give you a clue? Is this "second finding" related to the way a poet discovers beauty in things? Explain.

5. As an experimenter in language, Wilbur often used words in unusual ways; for example, *glides* and *valleys* in stanza 1. Find others in the poem and comment on the impression or image they create.

6. Although Wilbur used rhyme in this poem it was not conspicuous Why? Point out other ways in which he used sound in the poem.

Ogden Nash

The apparent light-heartedness of Ogden Nash's verse can be deceptive; the capricious, clever play of his mind often masks a quite serious concern with the follies and shams he sees in the world about him. To be sure, many of his short verses are simply extended puns or verbal jokes, but in his longer pieces he employs the sharp tools of the satirist to puncture the pompous and deflate the haughty.

Nash's two most distinctive stylistic devices are his frequent distortions of words to achieve rhyme and his exaggerated variations on otherwise regular rhythm patterns. The first of these allows him to poke fun indirectly at those who distort the facts to suit their own purposes. Together they provide him almost endless ways of achieving wry, unusual comic effects.

And Three Hundred and Sixty-Six in Leap Year

Some people shave before bathing,
And about people who bathe before shaving they are scathing,
While those who bathe before shaving,
Well, they imply that those who shave before bathing are mis-
    behaving.
Suppose you shave before bathing, well the advantage is that you
    don't have to make a special job of washing the lather off
    afterwards, it just floats off with the rest of your accumula-
    tions in the tub,   5
But the disadvantage is that before bathing your skin is hard and
    dry and your beard confronts the razor like a grizzly bear de-
    fending its cub.

Well then, suppose you bathe before shaving, well the advantage
    is that after bathing your skin is soft and moist, and your
    beard positively begs for the blade,
But the disadvantage is that to get the lather off you have to wash
    your face all over again at the basin almost immediately after
    washing it in the tub, which is a duplication of effort that
    leaves me spotless but dismayed.
The referee reports, gentlemen, that Fate has loaded the dice,
Since your only choice is between walking around all day with a
    sore chin or washing your face twice.   10
So I will now go and get a shave from a smug man in a crisp
    white coat,
And I will disrupt his smugness by asking him about his private
    life, does he bathe before shaving or shave before bathing,
    and then I will die either of laughing or of a clean cut throat.

1. What is Mr. Nash satirizing in this poem? Is it clearly stated or only
    implied? Explain.
2. In what way is the humor of the last line different from the humor of
    the rest of the poem? What added meaning does the title give?

The Terrible People

People who have what they want are very fond of telling people
    who haven't what they want that they really don't want it,
And I wish I could afford to gather all such people into a gloomy
    castle on the Danube and hire half a dozen capable Drac-
    ulas to haunt it.
I don't mind their having a lot of money, and I don't care how
    they employ it,
But I do think that they damn well ought to admit they enjoy it.
But no, they insist on being stealthy   5
About the pleasures of being wealthy,

And the possession of a handsome annuity
Makes them think that to say how hard it is to make both ends
    meet is their bounden duity.
You cannot conceive of an occasion
Which will find them without some suitable evasion.   10
Yes indeed, with arguments they are very fecund;°   full
Their first point is that money isn't everything, and that they
    have no money anyhow is their second.
Some people's money is merited,
And other people's is inherited,
But wherever it comes from,   15
They talk about it as if it were something you got pink gums
    from.
This may well be,
But if so, why do they not relieve themselves of the burden by
    transferring it to the deserving poor or to me?
Perhaps indeed the possession of wealth is constantly distressing,
But I should be quite willing to assume every curse of wealth if
    I could at the same time assume every blessing.   20
The only incurable troubles of the rich are the troubles that
    money can't cure,
Which is a kind of trouble that is even more troublesome if you
    are poor.
Certainly there are lots of things in life that money won't buy,
    but it's very funny—
Have you ever tried to buy them without money?

1. What reasons did the poet give for referring to the people in the
    poem as "terrible"? Why did he wish he were one of them?
2. What is the basis for the humor of the poem: irony, satire, or ridi-
    cule? How important is exaggeration to bringing out that humor?
    Find examples as evidence.
3. Which devices mentioned in the headnote did Nash use in this poem?

The Sea-Gull

Hark to the whimper of the sea-gull;
He weeps because he's not an ea-gull.
Suppose you were, you silly sea-gull,
Could you explain it to your she-gull?

The Parsnip

The parsnip, children, I repeat,
Is simply an anemic beet.
Some people call the parsnip edible;
Myself, I find this claim incredible.

Edouard

A bugler named Dougal MacDougal
Found ingenious ways to be frugal.
He learned how to sneeze
In various keys,
Thus saving the price of a bugle.

The Octopus

Tell me, O Octopus, I begs,
Is those things arms, or is they legs?
I marvel at thee, Octopus;
If I were thou, I'd call me Us.

A Caution to Everybody

Consider the auk;
Becoming extinct because he forgot how to fly, and could only
    walk.
Consider man, who may well become extinct
Because he forgot how to walk and learned how to fly before
    he thinked.

1. Even in these five short verses there is a satiric bite. In which ones can you find an implied criticism of human folly?
2. In what ways does the very compression of these poems add to their effectiveness? Point out likenesses and differences between these short verses and Nash's longer poems. What additional devices can you find in the verses?

GLOSSARY OF LITERARY TERMS

A

alliteration: the repetition of a consonant sound, usually at the beginning of two or more words in a line of verse or in a sentence:
> "Doom is darker and deeper than any sea-dingle."
> —W. H. Auden

allusion: a reference to some person, place, or event with literary, historical, or geographical significance.

analogy: a comparison of ideas or objects which are essentially different but which are alike in one significant way; for example, the analogy between the grasshopper and the man who lives only for the moment.

apostrophe: a figure of speech in which words are addressed to a person or thing—absent or present—or to a personified idea, such as death, truth, or nature:
> "O world, I cannot hold thee close enough!"
> —Edna St. Vincent Millay

assonance: the repetition in lines of verse of the same vowel sound accompanied by unlike consonant sounds, sometimes used in place of rhyme:
> "Bound to plow down a forest . . ."
> —Robinson Jeffers

atmosphere: the general over-all feeling of a literary work conveyed in large part by the setting and the mood.

B

ballad: a narrative that has sprung from unknown sources, has been transmitted by word of mouth (often altered in the process), and was intended to be sung.

> **ballad, folk:** a ballad which originated with the "folk" or common people. Its authorship is unknown.

> **ballad, literary:** a ballad composed by a known author who consciously imitated the stanza form, rhythm pattern, and rhyme scheme of the folk ballad. The story told may have originated with the "folk" and previously been transmitted by word of mouth.

blank verse: unrhymed verse that is generally written in iambic pentameter:

> "It takes the moon for this. The sun's a wizard
> By all I tell; but so's the moon a witch."
> —Robert Frost

C

cadence: the effect created by the rise and fall of the voice and by the emphasis and pause required by the meaning. In other words, the rhythm is not determined by a carefully planned combination of accented and unaccented syllables, as in traditional verse.

caesura: the main pause within a line of verse to indicate both the rhythm and the sense:

> "It was not dying: everybody died."
> —Randall Jarrell

characterization: the portrayal in a literary work of an imaginary person by what he says or does, by what others say about him or how they react to him, and by what the author reveals directly or through a narrator.

cliché: an expression used so often that it has lost its freshness and effectiveness.

climax: the point of highest interest or dramatic intensity. Usually it marks a turning point in the action, since the reader is no longer in doubt about the outcome.

coincidence: the chance occurrence of two events which take place at the same time.

colloquial: having the tone of familiar, everyday speech.

conflict: the struggle between two opposing forces, ideas, or beliefs, which form the basis of the plot. The conflict is resolved when one force—usually the protagonist—succeeds or fails in overcoming the opposing force or gives up trying.

connotation: the implied or suggested meaning of a word or expression through emotional, literary, or sound associations.

contrast: the bringing together of ideas, images, or characters to show how they differ and bring out meaning not clear if they stand alone.

couplet: two consecutive lines of verse, usually of equal length and rhyming together:

> "He gives his harness bells a shake
> To ask if there is some mistake."
> —Robert Frost

D

denotation: the literal dictionary meaning of a word or expression.

dialect: the speech that is characteristic of a particular region or of a class or group of people.

dialogue: the printed conversation between two or more characters in fiction, drama, or poetry.

didactic: morally instructive or intended to be so.

E

elegy: a poem of subjective or meditative nature, especially one of grief.

episode: a related group of incidents, or a major event, that comprises all or part of the main plot or, in a long work, is related to the main plot.

euphemism: a mild, inoffensive word or expression used in place of one that is harsh or unpleasant; for example, "to pass away" is a euphemism for "to die."

F

fable: a short tale, in prose or verse, that teaches a moral, often with animals or inanimate objects as characters.

figure of speech: the general term for a number of literary and poetic devices in which words or groups of words are used to create images in the mind or to make a comparison.

flashback: a device by which a writer interrupts the main action of a story, play, or poem to re-create a situation or incident of an earlier time as though it were occurring in the present.

foot: a combination of accented and unaccented syllables which make up a metrical unit. A foot may incorporate syllables from different words, and the foot divisions may cut across words, thus:
    "The cúr/tains dráwn / upón / unfríend/ly níght."

    foot, anapestic: a metrical unit consisting of two unaccented syllables followed by one accented syllable (interrúpt).

    foot, dactylic: a metrical unit consisting of one accented syllable followed by two unaccented syllables (dífferent).

    foot, iambic: a metrical unit consisting of one unaccented syllable followed by one accented syllable (abóve).

    foot, spondaic: a metrical unit consisting of two accented syllables in succession:
    "Some things that fly there be,—
    Bírds, hóurs, the bumble-bee . . ."
    —Emily Dickinson

foot, trochaic: a metrical unit consisting of one accented syllable followed by one unaccented syllable (prómise).

free verse: verse which does not conform to any fixed pattern. Such poetic devices as rhyme and rhythm occur only incidentally.

H

hyperbole: a figure of speech employing obvious exaggeration: for example, "His mind was a million miles away."

I

idiom: the language or manner of speaking that is typical of a particular region or group of people.

idyll: a poem or prose piece describing the simple pleasures of rural life.

image: a general term for any representation of a particular thing with its attendant and evocative detail. It may be a metaphor, a simile, or a straightforward description. An image may also have symbolic meaning.

irony: a mode of expression in which the author says one thing and means the opposite. The term also applies to a situation, or the outcome of an event (or series of events), that is contrary to what is naturally hoped for or expected.

J

juxtaposition: the placement of things side by side to bring out meaning not evident when they stand alone.

L

legend: a story that has come down from the past and that may have some basis in history.

locale: the particular place in which the action in a work of fiction occurs.

lyric: any short poem that seems to be especially musical and expresses, in most instances, the poet's clearly revealed thoughts and feelings.

M

metaphor: a figure of speech in which two things are compared without the use of *like* or *as*:

"Death is an elephant . . ."
—Vachel Lindsay

meter: the pattern of rhythm determined by the relationships between the accented and unaccented syllables in a line of poetry. Meter is established by the repetition of a dominant foot, such as iambic pentameter, a line of verse consisting of 5 iambs:

> "I célebráte mysélf, and síng mysélf . . ."
> —Walt Whitman

metrical line: a line of verse composed of one or more feet. The following names are used to identify the most common lines:

monometer: one foot	**pentameter:** five feet
dimeter: two feet	**hexameter:** six feet
trimeter: three feet	**heptameter:** seven feet
tetrameter: four feet	

monologue: a poem, or a passage in a drama, in which a single character or actor speaks alone and, usually, at some length.

mood: the frame of mind or state of feeling created by a piece of writing; for example, a skeptical mood or a sentimental mood.

moral: the lesson taught by a literary work.

N

narrative poem: a story told in verse form.

O

ode: a lengthy, dignified lyric poem expressing exalted or enthusiastic emotion, often about some person or occasion worthy of esteem.

onomatopoeia: the use of a word in which the sound suggests what the word designates (*splash, buzz, murmur*). This device enables the writer to express sense through sound.

P

paradox: a statement which seems on the surface contradictory, yet if interpreted figuratively, it involves an element of truth:

> "Much madness is divinest sense . . ."
> —Emily Dickinson

parody: a humorous imitation or burlesque of a serious piece of literature or writing.

pathetic fallacy: the ascribing to inanimate objects of those actions, qualities, and passions considered human. (For example: "a stubborn door.") The distinction between pathetic fallacy and personification or metaphor is not always clear. As a rule, though, the pathetic fallacy seems overdone.

pathos: that quality in prose or poetry that evokes in the reader a feeling of pity and compassion.

personification: a figure of speech in which places, things, animals, or ideas are endowed with human qualities:

> "The hills untied their bonnets . . ."
> —Emily Dickinson

Q

quatrain: a stanza consisting of four lines.

R

realistic: the faithful portrayal of people, scenes, and events as they are, not as the writer or artist would like them to be.

rhetorical question: a question that is asked for its dramatic effect and to which no answer is expected.

rhyme: the identity of sounds in accented syllables and of all vowel and consonant sounds following (*beautiful, dutiful*). The term *rhyme* is ordinarily used in the sense of end rhyme, the identity of sounds in words occurring at the end of matching lines of poetry.

> **rhyme, eye:**   the appearance, in close proximity, of two words which, because of their similar spellings, look alike but when pronounced do not sound alike (*heath and death*).

> **rhyme, feminine:**   a rhyming of matching lines of poetry in which the accented syllable is followed by one or more unaccented syllables which also rhyme:
>
>> "Tell them, dear, that if eyes were made for seeing,
>> Then Beauty is its own excuse for being . . ."
>> —Ralph Waldo Emerson

> **rhyme, internal:**   the rhyming of a word in the middle of a line of poetry with a word at the end of the line:
>
> "Once upon a midnight dreary, while I pondered weak and weary . . ."
> —Edgar Allan Poe

> **rhyme, masculine:**   a rhyming of matching lines of poetry in which the last syllable is accented:
>
>> "At midnight in the month of June,
>> I stand beneath the mystic moon."
>> —Edgar Allan Poe

rhyme, near: an approximate or imperfect rhyme:
"The hawthorn hedges in *bloom*,
When, serene in their ivory vessels,
The three wise Maries *come* . . ."
                                        —W. H. Auden

rhyme scheme: a fixed pattern of rhymes and also a fixed pattern of lines (stanza form).

rhythm: in poetry, the recurrence of accented and unaccented syllables in a regular, or nearly regular, pattern.

rhythm pattern: the basic movement of a line, stanza, or poem resulting from the choice and arrangement of the metrical units (feet). The rhythm pattern of a line containing five iambic feet is iambic pentameter, thus:
"And lúmber dówn the nárrow gábled stréet . . ."
                                        —Robert Lowell

romantic: the portrayal of people, scenes, and events as they impress the writer or artist or as he imagines them to be. A romantic work has one or more of the following characteristics: an emphasis on feeling and imagination; a love of nature; a belief in the individual and the common man; an interest in the past; the unusual, the unfamiliar, the bizarre or picturesque; a revolt against authority or tradition.

S

satire: any piece of writing which criticizes manners, individuals, or political and social institutions by holding them up to ridicule.

sensibility: the capacity of an author to respond intellectually and emotionally to what he experiences; his receptivity to impressions and keen intellectual awareness.

setting: the time and place in which the events in a narrative (prose or poetry) take place.

simile: a figure of speech in which a comparison is made between two objects essentially unlike but resembling each other in one or more respects. The comparison is indicated by *like* or *as*:
"Ice black *as* ebony"
                                        —Stephen Vincent Benét

soliloquy: a speech in prose or poetry that is delivered by a character when he is alone. Its purpose is to convey to the reader (or theater audience) additional information, or to reveal what the character thinks and feels.

sonnet: a poem consisting of fourteen lines, usually written in iambic pentameter and treating with a single idea or emotion.

    sonnet, Italian or **Petrarchan:**   a sonnet composed of an octave (eight lines) followed by a *sestet* (six lines). The rhyme scheme of the octave is abba abba; that of the sestet is cdc dcd. Poets frequently vary the scheme of the sestet.

    sonnet, Shakespearean: a sonnet composed of three quatrains and a couplet. The rhyme scheme is abab cdcd efef gg.

stanza: a group of lines of verse treated as a unit and separated from other units by a space.

style: the distinctive manner in which the writer uses language: his choice and arrangement of words.

suspense: a feeling of excitement, curiosity, or expectation about the outcome of a narrative (prose or poetry).

symbol: an object that stands for, or represents, an idea, belief, superstition, social or political institution, etc. A pair of scales, for example, is often a symbol for justice.

T

tale: a simple story that recounts a real or imaginary event.

theme: the idea, general truth, or commentary on life or people brought out through a literary work.

tone: the feeling conveyed by the author's attitude toward his subject and the particular way in which he writes about it.

tone of voice: the revelation of an author's feelings through his choice of words and images and through emphasis; for example: sarcastic, sentimental, flippant.

ABOUT THE POETS

W. H. Auden (1907-   ) was born in York, England, and attended Gresham's School, Holt, and Christ Church College, Oxford. While at Oxford, and later as a school teacher in England, he became associated with a group of poets who felt that only the creation of a new order could arrest what they considered the decay of middle-class society. In 1937 Auden drove an ambulance for the Spanish Loyalists, and in the same year was awarded the King's Poetry Medal. Two years later he came to the United States to deliver a series of lectures at universities and colleges. By 1940 he had published four volumes of poetry, a collection of prose fiction, and two anthologies; he had also published three plays, in collaboration with the British playwright Christopher Isherwood. The year after he received an award from the American Academy of Arts and Letters (1945), he became a United States citizen. He returned to England in 1956, where he held the position of Professor of Poetry at Oxford until 1961.

Auden enjoys the distinction—as does T. S. Eliot—of being considered both an English poet and an American poet. In 1948 he was awarded the Pulitzer Prize in Poetry and in 1953 the Bollingen Prize.

Edward Estlin Cummings (1894-1962), the future *enfant terrible* of American poetry, was the son of a Boston clergyman, who had once taught English at Harvard and who was to become pastor of the famous Old South Church. In 1915 Mr. Cummings was graduated from Harvard College and in 1916 he took his M.A. at the University. He joined the Ambulance Corps in World War I and later served in the American infantry. His first prose work, *The Enormous Room* (1922), is an account of his experiences and observations while in a French detention camp.

After the war Cummings divided his time between New York and Paris—writing and painting. *Tulips and Chimneys*, his first collection of verse, appeared in 1923. He received the Dial Award for distinguished service to American letters in 1925. He devoted his entire life to the making of poetry and, unlike many poets, earned his living solely through the reading of his poems or the sale of them. Most of them are now available in small volumes whose titles are often as unconventional as the poems they contain.

In 1952 Cummings returned to Harvard, his Alma Mater, as the Charles Eliot Norton Professor of Poetry. He was elected a member of the American Academy of Arts and Letters and, in 1957, received the Bollingen Prize in Poetry.

Hilda Doolittle (1886-1961), whose pen name was H. D., was born in Bethlehem, Pennsylvania and, after a varied schooling, entered Bryn Mawr College. Poor health forced her to withdraw at the end of her sophomore year, and during the next several years of convalescence she wrote children's stories, some of them published in a Presbyterian paper. In 1911 she sailed for Europe, intending to stay only for the summer. However, when she reached London, she became so interested in the literary movements which had attracted other American writers, particularly Ezra Pound, that she remained. Soon she became a unique and valuable member of the Imagist group and, in 1913, married Richard Aldington, who was also an Imagist. Together they made several translations of Greek and Latin poets. H. D.'s first collection of poems, *Sea Garden*, was published in 1916 in England, followed by a second volume, *Hymen*, in 1921. In the meantime, she and her husband separated and she returned to the United States. In less than a year she again went abroad, this time to Switzerland, where she remained, writing verse and studying Greek culture. Between 1916 and 1961 she published only four volumes of poetry, besides her *Collected Poems* (1925), but each poem was as carefully wrought as it was intensely original.

Robert Frost (1875-1963), who made poetry out of rural New England life, was born in San Francisco. After the death of his father, young Robert and his mother moved to Lawrence, Massachusetts, where they lived with his father's parents. When he graduated from high school, he shared the honor of being co-valedictorian with Elinor Miriam White, who became his wife in 1895. He spent a few months at Dartmouth College and two years at Harvard University but left without taking a degree. (In 1957 he was awarded honorary degrees by both Oxford and Cambridge.) For a time Frost tried varied occupations: farming, shoemaking, teaching, reporting—all of them to support his family. He had begun to write verse at fifteen, and had never ceased to write it. Regularly he sent his poems to the four leading magazines of that time, *Scribners, Harpers,* the *Century,* and the *Atlantic Monthly.* Just as regularly his poems were rejected.

In 1912, Frost sold the farm his grandfather had given him and, with his wife and children, went to England. Here, for the first time, he lived in a literary atmosphere, a friend of well-established poets. When *A Boy's Will,* Frost's first volume of poems, was published in England in 1913, it attracted some attention. The second volume, *North of Boston* (1914), added to his reputation. However, it was not until this volume was republished in the United States that Frost began to be widely known in his own country.

When Frost returned to America in 1915, he combined farming with college and university teaching. In later years he was in great demand as a lecturer and a reader of his poems. With each new volume of poems—including his most recent, *In the Clearing* (1962)—his reputation has grown until today he is recognized as one of America's greatest poets. He has received the Pulitzer Prize in Poetry four times: for *New Hampshire* (1924), *Collected Poems* (1931), *A Further Range* (1937), and *A Witness Tree* (1943).

Robinson Jeffers (1887-1962) was educated both in this country and abroad, devoting himself to such widely different subjects as medicine, forestry, zoology, and the classics. When he received a legacy from his uncle, he abandoned his academic pursuits to devote himself entirely to literature. After his marriage in 1913, he settled on a bluff overlooking Carmel Bay, California. Here he built Tor House from the granite stones he found on the beach, and here he lived a life of seclusion with his family. He also erected with his own hands the stone tower in which he did much of his writing. For his poetry he received several honorary degrees and was elected to membership in the American Academy of Arts and Letters. For his two plays *Medea* (1946) and *The Cretan Woman* (1954), he received the praise of New York drama critics. For *Hungerfield and Other Poems*, which was published in 1954, he was awarded the Pulitzer Prize.

Vachel Lindsay (1879-1931) was something of a Puritan, an artist, a missionary, and a vagabond. From his family in Springfield, Illinois, and from Hiram College in Ohio, he acquired a life-long devotion to Protestantism. From his mother, an energetic and religious woman, he received indulgent encouragement for his dreams of becoming "the disciple of beauty and civic virtue." After three years in college, he went first to Chicago and then to New York to study art. It was not his painting, however, that was destined to bring him fame; rather it was his rhythmic and resounding verse. His first book of poems, published in 1913, brought him national recognition. From a painter he now became a sort of wandering minstrel, tramping across the country and reciting his poetry to the people. For many years he lived on the slender income from these transcontinental tours. Finally, the constant strain of his travels and a growing sense of futility took their toll. Burdened by poor health and depressed by waning creative powers, he died by his own hand on December 5, 1931.

Amy Lowell (1874-1925) was as impressive in personality as she was in appearance, wealth, and prestige. She began her education at home under the guidance of her mother; she later attended private schools and traveled extensively in Europe and America. At the turn of the century she found herself unable to lead the idle life expected of an educated, well-to-do woman. Therefore, she turned to the study of literature, particularly classical and contemporary European poetry. During this time she was writing poetry herself, her first poem appearing in 1910, her first book of poems, in 1912. From 1913—when she joined the Imagist group in London—until her death in 1925, she wrote and lectured in behalf of the new poetry; these were years of recognition and success. She was invited to lecture at both Yale and Brown Universities. Her volume of poems *What's O'Clock*, published after her death, was awarded the Pulitzer Prize in 1925.

Archibald MacLeish (1892-   ) was born in Illinois and educated in Connecticut. In 1915 he received his A.B. from Yale and in 1919 his LL.B. from the Harvard Law School. After World War I, in which he rose to the rank of captain, he practiced law for three years before deciding, once and for all, to devote his life to poetry. With his family he moved to France where he lived for five years, traveling extensively, studying the French poets and the works of Eliot and Pound, and, in general, establishing himself as a poet in his own right. After his return to the United States in 1928, he continued his writing career and, in 1932, was awarded the Pulitzer Prize for his epic poem, *Conquistador*. During this time he also wrote articles on political and economic subjects for *Time* and *Fortune* magazines.

From 1939 to 1946 he held a variety of government posts. He was appointed Librarian of Congress, Director of the U. S. Office of Facts and Figures, Assistant Director of the Office of War Information, and Assistant Secretary of State; he was also chairman of the U. S. delegation to the London and Paris UNESCO conferences. In 1949 he was appointed Boylston Professor of Rhetoric and Oratory at Harvard University. In 1952 he received the Pulitzer Prize for his *Collected Poems, 1917-1952*. *J.B., A Play in Verse*, based on a biblical theme, was produced on Broadway in 1958 and was received enthusiastically by critics and audiences alike; the play was awarded the 1959 Pulitzer Prize in Drama.

Edgar Lee Masters (1869-1950) was a lawyer by vocation and a poet by avocation. Born in Kansas, he was brought up in central Illinois, the heart of the Lincoln country. Like his father before him, Masters became a lawyer, and for more than two decades he practiced his profession successfully in Chicago. Before 1915, the year in which *Spoon River Anthology* won him national acclaim, he had published eleven volumes of verse and prose, but they had earned him little attention either from the critics or from the public. In 1920 he gave up his law practice and devoted his full energies to writing. His later works include six novels, several plays, a study of Abraham Lincoln, a biography of Vachel Lindsay, and his own autobiography. Until his death in 1950, he resided, for the most part, in New York City.

Edna St. Vincent Millay (1892-1950) was born in Rockland, Maine, graduated from Vassar College in 1917, published her first book of poetry the same year, and went to New York to begin her work as a professional writer. A talented, vivacious girl, she quickly joined the Provincetown Players as an actress and as a playwright. The following quatrain, which she composed soon after her arrival in New York City, was immediately taken up by the Greenwich Village Bohemians as their "Psalm of Life":

> I burn my candle at both ends;
> It will not last the night.
> But ah my foes and oh my friends,
> It gives a lovely light.

In 1923 her volume of poems *The Harp-Weaver* was awarded the Pulitzer Prize. In 1926 she wrote the libretto for Deems Taylor's opera, *The King's Henchman*. When her sonnet sequence *Fatal Interview* was published in 1931, some critics condemned it for its confused emotions and imperfect syntax. Other critics compared it favorably with Shakespeare's sonnet sequence. During her life, Miss Millay received many honorary degrees and was elected to the American Academy of Arts and Letters.

Marianne Moore (1887-   ) was born in St. Louis, grew up in Pennsylvania, and graduated from Bryn Mawr in 1909 and from Carlisle Commercial College in 1910. For the next few years she taught stenography and other commercial subjects at the Carlisle Indian School. In 1921 she became an assistant in the New York Public Library system and held this position until 1925, when she became acting editor of *Dial*, a literary magazine. Volumes of her poetry appeared in 1921, 1924, 1935, 1936, 1941, and 1944; in 1951 her *Collected Poems* was awarded the Pulitzer Prize and the National Book Award. Since that time, she has published a translation of the Fables of La Fontaine (1954), a volume of essays (1955), and two volumes of verse (1956 and 1959). She lives in Brooklyn, New York, where for many years she has been an avid baseball fan and an enthusiastic collector of animal figurines.

Ogden Nash (1902-   ) has made a name for himself as a satirist with consistently witty verse. He belongs to what might be called the *New Yorker* school, urbane and intelligent, and distinctly East Coast.

He was born in Rye, New York, attended St. George's School, Rhode Island, and entered Harvard in the class of 1924. After one year of college, he taught briefly at a school in Rhode Island, and then came to New York, where he worked as a bond salesman, an advertising copywriter, and an editor. During the depression years he quit the business world to devote himself to writing. In addition to being the father of two children and eleven volumes of whimsical verse, he has written the lyrics for One Touch of Venus, a Broadway musical comedy. In 1950 he was elected a member of the National Institute of Arts and Letters.

Ezra Pound (1885-   ) was graduated from Hamilton College in 1905 and received a Master of Arts degree in romance languages from the University of Pennsylvania in 1906. The following year he went to Spain to gather materials for a doctoral thesis, and remained abroad for the next thirty-eight years. Rather than completing his academic studies, he wrote and published his first book of poetry (1908), translated medieval poetry, adapted Chinese poetry and Japanese Noh plays, organized the Imagist poets, and championed the writings of Eliot, Joyce, and Hemingway. In 1924 he settled in Rapallo, Italy where he unfortunately became associated with the so-called "liberals" who saw in Fascism a solution to the ills of the world. The volume of poems which he composed in Italy after the war, The Pisan Cantos, was awarded the 1949 Bollingen Prize for Poetry.

Edwin Arlington Robinson (1869-1935) grew up in the town of Gardiner, Maine, which was to become the "Tilbury Town" of his later poems. His youth and early education were marred by severe emotional strains: the decline of his father, the sickness and debts of his older brothers, the tragic death of his mother, and the loss of his patrimony during the depression of the nineties. After two years at Harvard (1891-1893), he returned to Gardiner to begin a long career of writing. Six years later he moved to New York where he held a variety of jobs, including the one which Theodore Roosevelt—an enthusiastic admirer—secured for him at the New York Customs House. In 1910, the year he gave up this job, his fourth volume of poems was published. Not until 1916, however, did he receive general recognition as a poet, and then largely as a result of the superb volume The Man Against the Sky.

Robinson never sought to advertise himself as a poet by public lectures or public readings. His devotion to his art was, according to one critic, as "whole-hearted as that of Wordsworth or Keats." Nevertheless, he eventually won both praise and honors: the Pulitzer Prize three different times and election to membership in the National Academy of Arts and Letters.

Carl Sandburg (1878-   ) was the son of poor Swedish immigrants. As a youth, he worked more than he attended school. He drove a milk wagon, swept floors in a barbershop, shifted scenery in a theater, and operated a truck at a brick kiln. At the age of seventeen he headed west, working when he had to but mostly listening to the men talk and learning the songs the people sing. After serving in the Sixth Illinois Infantry in the Spanish-American War, he attended Lombard College, where he first acquired his interest in writing. He did not, however, make writing a career until 1909, when he became a reporter and, later, a journalist. The publication of *Chicago Poems* in 1915 established him as a significant American poet. Later volumes added to his reputation, among them storybooks for children and the first comprehensive collection of musical Americana, *The American Songbag*. The last was the fruit of years of collecting and traveling about the country, reciting his poems, and singing to the accompaniment of his guitar. In 1926 he published the first of a six-volume biography of Abraham Lincoln, which was awarded the Pulitzer Prize in History. For *Complete Poems* (1950), he received the Pulitzer Prize in Literature.

Wallace Stevens (1879-1955) was educated at Harvard University and the New York University Law School, and was admitted to the bar in 1940. Except for one year as a newspaper reporter, he carried on a general law practice until 1916, when he joined the legal staff of an accident and indemnity company in Hartford, Connecticut. The first evidence of his poetic talent was the publication of several of his poems in *Poetry*, the magazine established by Harriet Monroe in Chicago. Not until 1923, however, did his poems appear in a single volume, entitled *Harmonium*. Although few copies were sold, this volume was hailed by many critics as one of the finest ever published in the United States. By 1937 Mr. Stevens had not only risen to the position of vice-president in the Hartford company, but had also published three more volumes of poetry. The combination of two such different careers—successful businessman and poet—is rare.

Unlike most poets, Stevens wrote most of his verse after he was forty, with his later volumes as distinguished as his first. In 1949 he received Yale University's Bollingen Award, and in 1951 the National Book Award. When *Collected Poems* was published in 1954, he was awarded the Pulitzer Prize in Poetry. The last honor shown him before his death in 1955 was election to membership in the American Academy of Arts and Letters.

Richard Wilbur (1921-   ) has published four volumes of verse since his graduation from Amherst College in 1942. Following service with the 36th Infantry Division in World War II, he took his M.A. at Harvard University and taught English there until 1954. In 1952 he received a Guggenheim Fellowship and in 1954 he was awarded the Prix de Rome of the American Academy of Arts and Letters. For his volume of poems *Things of This World* he was awarded the Pulitzer Prize and the National Book Award for 1956. Mr. Wilbur also wrote the lyrics for the musical version of *Candide*, which was produced on Broadway in 1957. He is currently Associate Professor of English at Wellesley College.

Wilbur's poetry reflects his wide reading, especially in the works of his contemporaries. Each new volume shows an increasing range of poetic skill and a greater perfection of his distinctly personal style.

William Carlos Williams (1883-1963) was a practicing physician as well as a poet. His rich experiences as a doctor in a small industrial town near Paterson, New Jersey provided him with much of the subject matter for his poems. The vigor and zest of his poetic style can, in some measure, be traced to his mixed ancestry: English, French, Spanish, and Jewish. His major poetic work, *Paterson* (1946-1951), is a four-volume chronicle into which he claimed to have poured "the whole knowable world about me." In addition to poetry, Dr. Williams wrote plays, novels, short stories, and books of literary criticism. In 1950 he was elected to the National Institute of Arts and Letters, and in 1953 shared with Archibald MacLeish the Bollingen Prize for Poetry.

Elinor Wylie (1887-1928), a novelist as well as a poet, began to write verse at Miss Baldwin's School in Bryn Mawr, Pennsylvania before she was ten. She completed her education at the Holton Arms School in Washington and for a while enjoyed the social life of a debutante. Married at twenty and a widow at twenty-four, she then married Horace Wylie, whom she later divorced. Her writing career began with the publication of *Nets to Catch the Wind* (1921), her first volume of poems, which the Poetry Society of America chose as the best verse of the year. About this time she met William Rose Benét, a poet, critic, and novelist, married him in 1923, and began the first of four historical novels. For each she did an enormous amount of research, deriving great satisfaction from gathering facts and weaving them into a romantic and brilliant fabric. Each sentence of her prose she set down slowly and with precision. Her poetry she penned out quickly and without erasure, for the composing of it had already taken place in her head.

A second volume of Miss Wylie's verse was published in 1923, and a third in 1928, when she was in England. Doctors had warned her that she must not overtax herself, for she suffered from high blood pressure.

She worked more industriously than ever, however, producing a sonnet series of forty poems. When she returned to New York in December to arrange for the publication of the series, she died of a sudden stroke of paralysis. She was only forty-three. The sonnet series was published posthumously, as was her *Collected Poems*, which were assembled by William Rose Benét.